The Sleeping Beauty

A Pantomime

David Cregan

Music by Brian Protheroe

Samuel French—London
New York—Sydney—Toronto—Hollywood

SAMUEL FRENCH LTD, 52 Fitzroy Street, London, W1P 6JR, or their authorized agents, issue licences to amateurs to give performances of this play on a payment of a fee. **This fee is subject to contract and subject to variation at the sole discretion of Samuel French Ltd.**

Licences are issued subject to the understanding that it shall be made clear in all advertising matter that the audience will witness an amateur performance; and that the names of the authors of the plays shall be included on all announcements and on all programmes.

The publication of this play must not be taken to imply that it is necessarily available for performance by amateurs or professionals, either in the British Isles or overseas. Amateurs intending production must, in their own interests, make application to Samuel French Ltd or their authorized agents, for consent before starting rehearsals or booking a theatre or hall.

The Professional Rights in this play are controlled by MARGARET RAMSAY LTD, 14a Goodwin's Court, St Martin's Lane, London WC2N 4LL.

ISBN 0 573 06472 5

THE SLEEPING BEAUTY

First presented at the Theatre Royal, Stratford East, London on 5th December, 1983, with the following cast of characters:

Helpful 1	Oliver Pierre
Helpful 2	Ian Bartholomew
King Robert	Martin Duncan
Queen Cynthia	Christine Pilgrim
Archbishop	James Walker
Glynis, Fairy Godmother	Jo Warne
Blanche, Fairy Godmother	Isabelle Lucas
Roxy, Fairy Godmother	Linda Dobell
Nurse Hallowpenny	Gorden Kaye
Maultash, Fairy Godmother	Darlene Johnson
Rose	Joanne Whalley
Prince Claude/Crispin	Stephen Persaud

Directed by Philip Hedley and Celia Bannermann

Designed by Gemma Jackson

Musical Direction by Colin Sell

The setting can be as elaborate or as simple as desired. In the original production a standing set of the Palace courtyard was used with various trucks for the thrones etc being brought on to effect the scene changes. Maultash's "cloud" was a truck and several front cloths were used, too

CHARACTERS

King Robert
Queen Cynthia
Rose, their daughter
Nurse Hallowpenny
Crispin, the Princess's friend
Roxy
Blanche } Fairy Godmothers
Glynis
Maultash, the wicked Godmother
Helpful Man 1
Helpful Man 2
Archbishop
Claude, the Prince
Courtiers
Roses

Crispin and Prince Claude can be doubled. The Courtiers can be extras or can be played by cast members to keep the number of actors required to a minimum

MUSICAL NUMBERS

The piano / vocal score is available from Samuel French Ltd

ACT I

1	Welcome Hymn	The Company
2	Godmums' Jingle	Godmothers
3	No-one Ever Loves You Like a Godmum	Godmothers
4	Nanny, Where's Your Bosom?	Nurse Hallowpenny and Chorus
5	Maultash Is A Wicked Fairy	King and Chorus
6	She's A Fool	Nurse Hallowpenny and Godmums
7	Song of the Names	Archbishop and Company
8	(She's Got) Blue Eyes	Roxy, Blanche and Glynis
9	Tick-Tock	Godmothers
10	Grandmother's Footsteps	Crispin, 1, 2, Rose, Archbishop and Audience
11	To Be Me	Rose
12	The Gutbuster	Nurse Hallowpenny and Company

ENTR'ACTE

13	We Need a Royal Personage-Oh	Godmothers, 1, 2 and Prince
14	Sleeping Beauty's Boy	Godmothers, 1, 2 and Prince

ACT II

15	Dream of a Dream	King, Queen, Nurse Hallowpenny and Rose
16	Don't Be Brave	1 and 2
17	Maultash's Revenge	Maultash
18	Prince of the Dream	Roses and Prince
19	Will It Come True?	Prince
20	Just Good Friends	Company

PROLOGUE*

King Robert and the pregnant Queen Cynthia have been wandering about in the foyer as the Audience arrive. The two Helpful Men, 1 and 2, have also been welcoming the Audience

As the House Lights go down 1 and 2 make their way to the stage. The front cloth is down

1 Can we lower the lights please?

The House Lights are taken out completely

    Silence for the King!
2 Silence! Quiet!
1 Silence for His Majesty!
2 Silence. Quiet. Hush
1 We're two very helpful people. We're members of the Theatre Staff, and we really belong down there.
2 But we've come up here to give a hand because we're so very, very helpful.
1 Very helpful to everyone, but especially big wigs.
2 And as there are no bigger wigs than Royals ...

1
2 } (*together*) Silence for His Majesty the King!

The King comes on in his nightgown and nightcap. He is a very nervous man at all times

King (*to 1 and 2*) Quiet! The baby's due any minute!
1 (*in a whisper*) Quiet! Hush!
2 Quiet for the new baby, not yet delivered.
King (*nervously*) She's in there having it now.

They all listen again

    Go on, Cynthia, push.
Queen (*off*) I am doing, Robert.
King Good. (*To 1 and 2*) Is the whole nation waiting with baited breath?
1 I'll go and see Your Majesty.
King Yes, do.
1 (*calling as he goes*) Is the whole nation waiting with baited breath?

    1 exits

King (*to the audience*) We've been wanting an heir to the throne for ages, (*to 2*) haven't we?

---

2 Yes, sire.

King (*to the audience*) Everybody's pleased as punch (*to 2*) aren't they?

2 Yes, sire.

King (*nervously*) They are, aren't they?

2 Yes, sire.

King And the guns and bells and everything are ready to celebrate with?

2 Yes, sire.

1 enters

1 The nation *is* waiting with baited breath Your Majesty, very anxious, very excited.

King And all the guns and bells are ready so (*turning to the frontcloth*) hurry up! I can't stand the strain any longer!

1 Hurry up for His Majesty!

2 Get born for His Majesty!

1 Hurry up out into the world for His Majesty!

There is a sudden bellowing of infant cries

King That's it! That's a baby! I recognize the sound!

1 ⎫
2 ⎬ (*together*) Oh, congratulations. Oh, well done!

King (*pleased*) I used to be a worried old King, and now I'm a worried old father as well.

1 ⎫
2 ⎬ (*together*) Marvellous. Wonderful. You'll never regret it, I'm sure.

King Thank you. Do I know you, by the way?

1 Two very, very helpful members of the Theatre Staff.

2 From out there.

King Oh.

1 But it's more fun up here, so we've just accepted your offer of a job.

King Oh good. I'm so glad. Cynthia, turn off the crying, will you. It isn't very pretty.

Queen (*off*) I can't, Robert.

King (*as he goes*) Cynthia? Stop the crying.

The King exits

Queen (*off*) I can't!

1 Bells!

2 Guns!

1 Welcome to the baby!

2 Rejoice!

Bells and guns and general crashing is heard

Let's have the choir here, for the King.

1 Singing. Flags.

2 All that sort of thing.

1 Is it a boy?

Prologue

King (*off*) No, it's a girl.

$\left.\begin{array}{c} \mathbf{1} \\ \mathbf{2} \end{array}\right\}$ (*together*) A princess! Delicious!

A triumphal, antiphonal anglican sort of sound starts, with bells and guns, fitting, if possible the 1812 Overture

ACT I

The Royal Nursery

At the moment all is concealed by a flag-waving set of Courtiers in night attire. 1 and 2 are also there, but not in night attire. The Company prepare to sing Song 1 which is rather holy and accompanied by bangs and bells and the persistent crying of the Princess

1 Your Majesty. The nation is ready to congratulate you

Song 1: Welcome Hymn

Company   Welcome to the newborn princess,
Welcome to the girl of girls.
Star of stars, and joy of joys, and
Flower of flowers, and pearl of pearls.

Thus our hopes have been rewarded
Dreams fulfilled and all of that,
Well done, people, wondrous, super,
Let's hope nothing
Now falls flat.
Welcome! Welcome! Well—come!
Hosanna and Halleloooh!

During the last part of the song the baby's crying has got louder and louder, until the King bursts in, followed by the Queen

They hold the baby and pass it round so that it keeps coming back to them. It cries throughout, only stopping when indicated

King Oh Cynthia, please!
Queen (*distraught*) She goes on and on, Robert, that's all she does, and I can't do anything about it.
King Well, I've got to rule the country tomorrow.
Queen Well, I know.
King I've got to sign things and smile and pass a few laws.
Queen I know.
King And how am I going to do that when my daughter keeps me awake all night?
Queen Well. I've got to be nice to all those mayors and mayoresses, and thank those little girls for all those flowers, and ride in that awful draughty coach.
King Yes, I know.
Queen And I'm miserable as sin, and *I've* given birth to her.

King Yes, I know.
Queen (*crying*) It's too bad, because we're all supposed to be so happy.
King We are happy.
1
2 } (*together*) Yes, we are. Happy, everyone. Happy, happy, happy. Come along.
Courtier Who are they?
King (*to the Queen*) There, there, there.
1
2 } (*together*) There, there, there.

1 and 2 get the Audience doing this. The baby cries louder

King Quiet! I am sorry. It's very nice to feel supported——
Queen Oh, it is.
King But what we need is silence.
Queen Peace.
King A good night's sleep.
Courtier A nanny.

There is a stunned silence, suppressed excitement

King A what?
Courtier A nanny. A nursemaid. One of those people who gets up in the middle of the night, and takes her to the zoo, and wipes her nose, and stops her eating lollipops.
King What a stupendous, multicoloured ice-cream of an idea.
Queen But what will people say, Robert, if I don't bring her up myself?
King Now I've made a queen of you it doesn't matter what they say. Who will get me a nanny?
Courtier (*at first loudly, then whispered*) Ahem! Sire. The baby's gone quiet.

It has, in the arms of the Courtier who is speaking

King What?

The Courtier mouths so as not to wake the baby

Speak up. Oh, the baby's gone quiet.
1
2 } (*together*) Sh. Sh, everyone, sh for the baby. Very quiet, now, please for the baby.
Courtier (*to 1 and 2*) Shh!

Offended, 1 and 2 obey

King Right. Into the cot with it.
Queen Shh!
King Me?
Queen Sh. Yes.
King Sh.

1 and 2 are very busy clearing the way to the cot. The Courtier holding the baby is stepping tip toe

Courtier (*holding the baby*) She's ever so pretty, isn't she?

King Sh!
Queen Sh!
1 Sh!
2 Sh!
All (*in rapid fire, individually*) Sh!
Courtier I was only saying—
All (*together*) Sh!
King Careful now, careful.

The King is signalling the Courtier along like a man bringing an aeroplane down on to an aircraft carrier. 1 and 2 scuttle about moving grains of dust, furniture, people

Mind. Take care. Lay her down very carefully if you want to be sure of next week's wages.

At the last moment, as the Princess is put into her pram, she screams

Courtier (*desperate*) It wasn't my fault.
Queen Oh, Robert, it's so awful, what'll we do?
King Go and get a nanny! Go and find one now and bring her to the throne room first thing in the morning.
1 Certainly, Your Majesty.
2 Absolutely, Your Majesty.
1
2 } (*together*) Yes.

Queen Who are they?
King (*with sudden strength*) I don't know, but they'd better find a nanny or I'll have them forcibly fed on rancid butter and old face flannels. Cynthia, that daughter of yours is more trouble than she's worth!
Queen She's not just *my* daughter, Robert.
King (*reverting to his normal nervousness*) No dear, nor she is. I'd forgotten. Now let's try and get a good night's sleep.

Everyone exits

Courtier (*as he goes*) Is this the best of family life?

The Lights fade to a Black-out

SCENE 2

The Throne Room. Early dawn

Glynis, Blanche and Roxy, the Fairy Godmothers, enter in a shaft of light. Glynis is quite large and middle-aged; Roxy is young and inexperienced and Blanche is motherly and middle-aged

Glynis Before any more happens, you have to know that we are the Fairy Godmothers.
Blanche And we are important.

Roxy We're really, really very important, actually. And we're nice too.

Blanche And sensible.

Roxy Well—

Glynis Now, once the King and Queen get settled with their baby, they will have a christening to give it a name, because that is what everyone does.

Roxy And we always go to christenings, don't we, girls.

Blanche Yes.

Roxy And some of us get really, really excited.

Glynis Are you saying something about me?

Roxy I just meant we all have a good time, that's all.

Blanche As Fairy Godmothers, we bestow virtues on children. That is all you need to know about us.

Glynis Yes. For example, I'm going to make the Princess nice and rich. (*Pirouetting*) My name is Glynis.

Roxy And I'm going to make her really, really beautiful. (*Pirouetting*) My name is Roxy.

Blanche I will make her wise. My name is Blanche.

Glynis And probably we'll sing this little song to make everything proper, the way Fairy Godmothers should.

Song 2: Godmums' Jingle

Godmothers (*together* *demurely*)	We are going to bless you With joy your whole life through We will make you happy Whatever you may do.

Roxy There, isn't that sweet?

Glynis Actually, we do sometimes go a bit further.

Blanche Glynis?

Roxy Well we do, what with champagne and everything.

Glynis The fact is, we're absolutely bursting with love for everyone, aren't we girls?

Blanche ⎫
Roxy ⎭ (*together*) Yes

Song 3: No-One Ever Loves You Like a Godmum

Godmothers (*singing*)	No-one ever loves you like a Godmum. No-one ever cares so much for quite so long. Others dry your tears, And calm away your fears, But Godmums make things right When they are wrong. No-one does such magic as a Godmum, Waving off the weariness and strife. When days are running out of joy She'll fill them up again, and boy! She'll twinkle back the starlight In your life.

No-one ever glitters like a Godmum.
No-one ever had such Father Xmas charms.
She may be not be much
At keeping house and such
But magic moments fountain from her arms.

No-one else loves laughter like a Godmum,
The airy fairy girl who's all surprise,
So when the sky's completely black
And happiness just won't come back
She lights the love of living in your eyes.

The Godmothers execute a dance

No-one else loves laughter like a Godmum,
The airy fairy girl who's such a wow.
So when the sky's completely black
And happiness just won't come back,
When sorrow's making wrinkles in your brow,
Just trust a fairy Godmum now

1 and 2 enter after the song

1 Here's the nursemaid. We've found the nursemaid.
Glynis What?
2 This way, Nanny. (*To the Fairy Godmothers*) Will you leave?
Glynis Us?
1 Please.
Roxy Let's go where we can keep an eye on things secretly.
Glynis The Princess is our responsibility.
Blanche They'll never cope without us.

The Godmothers hide behind the thrones

1 Thank you.
2 Really, this place is so badly run.
1 Nanny! Nanny!
2 This way, Nanny!

Nurse Hallopenny enters. She is large, commanding and used to taking charge. She carries several suitcases

Nurse Are you talking to me?
1 }
2 } (*together*) Yes, we are, yes.
Nurse Well, the word is "please".
2 What word?
Nurse The nice bright little word that makes me think you're a nice bright little boy, and not a nasty rude little man (*To the Audience*) Hello.
2 Eh?
Nurse Is he a nasty rude little man?
1 No, I'm not, I'm not.

Nurse In that case you can say please.

1 and 2 practise saying "please"

That's better (*To the Audience*) Palaces aren't what they were. Look at that throne.

1 It's a nice throne.

2 Yes, it's lovely throne.

Nurse Then dust it.

1 Us?

Nurse Yes you. It's a trap for germs.

1⎫
2⎭ (*together*) A trap for germs. Bad for princesses. Must dust straight away. Very good, Nanny. Absolutely, Nanny. (*They dust the throne*)

Nurse Good boys. Now then, where is this princess?

The Archbishop, a tall, thin man, enters, wearing mitre and robes

The Light is more like morning now

Archbishop Oh. Are you the Nursemaid?

Nurse Yes. I am the famous Nurse Hallowpenny, nanny to the influential, never known to fail. Who are you?

Archbishop I'm the Archbishop.

Nurse Let's see your hands then.

Archbishop My what?

1⎫
2⎭ (*together*) Hands. Hands, come on show us your hands.

Archbishop Why? (*He shows his hands*)

1 She's a nanny, that's why.

2 A nanny.

Nurse Filthy. Ears?

1⎫
2⎭ (*together*) Ears. Come along. Let's see your ears.

Nurse Ditch-like. You could grow artichokes in there. I can see this place needs a shake up. Usual thing, I suppose. Too much money, incompetent parents, always the same with Royalty. (*She beams on the Audience*) I must say, it's good to see some good, sensible people out there. I may need you if everything is really as sloppy here as it looks.

The King and Queen enter and sit on their thrones. Several Courtiers enter with them

King (*attracting Nurse's attention*) Ahem!

Nurse What are you, the King or something?

King Yes.

Nurse Who said you could sit down?

King I'm the King. Nothing happens till I sit down. Who are you?

Nurse I'm Nurse Hallowpenny, and I've come to bring up your child. Where is she?

Queen I don't want her to go near the child, Robert! I've got a book, I'll be able to manage!

Nurse The mother?

King Yes.

Nurse Typical. All sugar and spice before you got married, wet as a dead snail now you've got a screaming infant. Where is it?

1 ⎫
2 ⎭ (*together*) Here, Nurse Hallowpenny. We'll get it, Nurse Hallow-penny. (*They start to leave*)

Nurse (*indicating her luggage*) Take that to my quarters. I shall be staying.

1 and 2 dash out, taking Nurse's luggage with them

Queen It's going to be like this all the time now, Robert. Nothing but chivvying the monarch.

King But there'll be sleep, Cynthia. D'you remember sleep?

1 and 2 come back with the baby screaming and with a folding table and things for the nappy change

Nurse Ah. Ahh. Ahh. (*She picks up the baby, whose cries subside to a gentle grizzle, and shows her to the Audience*) Who's uncomfy womfy? (*She lays the baby on the table*) Who needs a little changey nappy waps, then?

The baby's cries increase a little

A little changey nappy waps?

Nurse takes off the nappy, cooing nonsense to the baby. The crying goes down slightly. People peer

There. Who's going to take away dirty nappy waps for nanny panny?

People back away

You're going to take dirty nappy waps for nanny panny.

Nurse throws the wet nappy to a Courtier who squeaks and catches it. 1 and 2 are amused. There is more cooing nonsense

And who's going to take *one* little bit of cotton wool. (*She flicks a bit of cotton wool that she has used for cleaning at 1*) And who's going to take another bit of cotton wool. (*She flicks the second piece*) Now powder wowder for my little gurgly wurgly chubby chops, and a cosy clean nappy wap in a tricey wicey round the softy bot—

All are crowding round to look. Much gurgling and giggling from the baby

That's it. (*There is a very quick replacement of nappy*) And up for windies for nanny panny. Windies for nanny panny.

A huge burp is heard. Someone receives something in the eye

All Ah.

Gurgles of glee from the baby

All that windies to pop out? Shouldn't've been there at all, should it. (*She looks at the Queen*)

The Queen looks distressed

(*Giving the baby the bottle*) And here's some lovely drinky minky for the little lady love, and then more windies and then long, long sleepies.
King Oh, well done.

There is applause from all

D'you do this all the time? Bringing up babies?
Nurse Of course, I do. I'm famous for it. And I remember every one of them.

The Godmothers peer out from behind the throne

Song 4: Nanny, Where's Your Bosom

(*Singing*)
Young, strong, and beautiful,
Heroes yet to be,
Learn the little ways of life
By holding hands with me.
How I adore them when
They call out in the night,
"Nanny, where's your bosom,
To rest on till it's light."

Princess and Noblemen,
Lions young and bold,
Telling me their secret loves
Like shining knights of old—
I'll always hear them when
They call out in the fight,
"Nanny, where's your bosom,
To rest on till it's light."

When time dismisses me
No more at their side,
Still to wonders yet unborn
I'll flow like a restless tide.
Their cry will always reach me
Mid the angels bright,
"Nanny, where's your bosom,
To rest on till it's light."

The final two lines are repeated three times

After the song Nurse exits with the baby followed by the Godmothers

Queen She's terribly forceful, Robert.
King Well, we could do with more forcefulness around the palace, really. Bracing, I think we'll find it. Anyway, now that's settled, look at this. (*He produces a large scroll*)
Queen What is it?

King (*delightedly*) It's the list of people we're going to ask to the christening.

Queen Oh Robert! In the Crystal Christening Hall?

King Yes dear, in the Crystal Christening Hall.

All Ah, the Crystal Christening Hall. Oh what a treat, oh goodness.

Queen There'll be wine, and cakes and the Archbishop in his hat and lots and lots of Fairy Godmothers.

King (*doubtfully*) Oh I don't know about them. There's some very funny people doing it nowadays, you know.

Queen You mean that horrible one called—Maultash.

All Sh!

Queen You wouldn't ask her, Robert.

King Of course not. It's just you never know where you are with her.

Queen We'll just ask the nice ones.

King Yes, I'll go and see to it.

The King and Queen begin to walk slowly to the exit, looking very nervous and worried

Queen Nothing'll go wrong, will it?

King No, of course it won't, will it?

Queen No, I'm sure it won't, will it?

King I don't think so, will it? No, I'm sure.

Queen No.

They have nearly gone, but turn back nervously to listen to the following conversation

1 Who's this er—this Maultash, then?

All Sh.

Archbishop Haven't you heard?

King She lives on an Awful Cloud.

Queen She's an awful person.

2 Oh.

The King and Queen run back

King Listen while we tell you.

Queen And make sure nobody else is listening.

Song 5: Maultash Is A Wicked Fairy

King (*singing*)   Maultash is a wicked fairy,
Maultash lives a life of crime,
Maultash has a chest that's hairy,
Maultash washes up in slime.

She puts fags out on the carpet,
Blocks the S bend in the sink,
On hot days she bares her arm-pit,
Flies in millions die of stink.

Chorus   She's bad,
             She's got no manners,
             She's poison, she's a bore,
             The very end.
             We've had
             A hundred spanners
             In our works, because she likes to drive us
             Screaming round the bend.

             Always, always cheats at games and
             Never, never says what's true,
             Then she calls out horrid names and
             Tells the teacher it was you.

             Furthermore, she thinks it's funny
             When she burps right in your face.
             Worse, she nicks your pocket money,
             For she really hates the human race,
             Human race,
             Human race.

Repeat first chorus and first verse

1 No Maultash.
2 No Maultash.
King ⎱
Queen ⎰ (*together*) Yuk, yuk, yuk, yuk, yuk.

Black-out

SCENE 3

The Royal Nursery

Nurse Hallowpenny puts a christening robe on the baby, and then lays it in a marvellous perambulator affair

Nurse Who's going to be the prettiest princess ever? Oh, such a pretty, pretty girl.

Nurse hugs the baby and it gurgles

That's it. Now, all ready to have your names given at the christening, down in the Crystal Christening Hall? Oh, yes.

Roxy enters with a baby in a cardboard box. She is in obvious disguise as an old lady. She coughs

Hello, who might you be?
Roxy I'm an old and very frail wood cutter's wife.
Nurse Really? Wandering round the palace just like that?

Roxy Yes.

Nurse Find any good trees to cut down in the corridors? Ha, ha. (*To the Audience*) They expect you to believe anything in this place.

Roxy It's my husband who cuts down trees. I find homes for babies.

Nurse Oh yes?

Roxy I'm told you love them, but haven't managed to have any of your own.

Nurse (*tartly*) I will one day. One day I'll find my own true love and get married and have a family.

Roxy To be on the safe side, why not have this which I found on the back doorsteps of the palace and who would make a really really good friend for the Princess later on?

Nurse peers in at the baby

Glynis and Blanche pop their heads round the scenery

Blanche It is Roxy, isn't it?

Glynis Yes, and I taught her. I used to be famous for my old wood cutter's wife. "Say friend, can you help an old wood cutter's wife who . . ."

Blanche Glynis! What's she doing?

Glynis Well, she said she had this feeling that the Princess was going to need a friend, that's all.

Nurse I don't know. I don't bring up any old back door stepchild you know. I'm nanny to the influential. (*To the Audience*) People do try to take advantage.

Roxy But he's ever so, ever so lovely.

Coos and gurgles are heard from the box

Nurse Fleas? Rickets? Lice even?

Roxy Certainly not!

Nurse No? Oh—you all know how to catch me on my soft side, don't you. You know I always fall in love with babies. Let me have a closer look. (*She takes him out and cuddles him*) He's a pet. He's just a bundle of joy.

Godmothers (*together*) Aah!

Song 6: She's A Fool

Nurse
None of it's going to be easy,
One at a time is my rule,
But he just has to dribble,
And Oh! I can't quibble,
Where babes are concerned I'm a fool.
His origins seem rather sleazy,
But turning him out is so cruel,
And look how he blows
All that stuff down his nose—
I'm a fool, I'm a fool, I'm a fool.

Chorus

Godmothers	She's a fool
Nurse	(I'm a fool)
Godmothers	She's a fool
Nurse	(Such a fool)
Godmothers	We're happy to say she's a fool
Nurse	(Just a fool)
Godmothers	One peep at his dimple and she becomes simple
	A fool, a glorious fool!
Godmothers	(*underneath the next verses*)
	Who's a coochy little di-dums
	Who's a googa baba loo *etc*
Nurse	Two little friends for each other,
	Two little babes full of drool,
	Such slurpings and sloppings,
	And burpings and poppings,
	It's paradise—Oh, what a fool.
	They'll grow up like sister and brother,
	And trot hand in hand off to school,
	In the midwinter freeze,
	They'll go pink at the knees,
	I'm a fool I'm a fool, I'm a fool.
Godmothers	She's a fool, she's a fool,
	We're happy to say she's a fool,
	One peep at his dimple,
	And she's become simple,
	A fool, a glorious fool!

The Godmothers start to exit

Glynis I hope you know what you were doing, Roxy.
Roxy I just had this feeling that's all.
Blanche You do the old wood cutter's wife very well these days.
Glynis I taught her.
Nurse Has the boy a name?
Roxy Crispin. His name's Crispin.

The Godmothers exit

Nurse Well, if you'll just take him round to the nursery and put him down while—oh! Where's she gone? Hello? Hello?

The Archbishop enters

Archbishop Hello. Now let's get this christening on the road, shall we. And get rid of that rubbish.
Nurse It's not rubbish, it's Crispin.

1 and 2 enter and blow a fanfare—a horrible sound—to take us into Scene 4

SCENE 4

The Crystal Christening Room. A vast, magical looking room

Everyone, except 1 and 2, are onstage. The Archbishop is holding the baby

Queen And we haven't asked Maultash?
King No.
Queen You're sure.
King Yes.
Queen D'you think she'll mind?
King Yes, but it's too late now.

Song 7: Song of the Names

Archbishop We are gathered here today
(singing) To help this princess on her way.
Therefore all the world shall know
These the names that we bestow.

The names can be sung by various groups of people, as desired

Henrietta, Margaretta, Cora, Kay,
Getrude, Isabella, Martha, May,
Jean, Jilly, Georgiana, June, Justine,
Milly, Molly, Mandy, Mary-Beth, Marlene.

Hannah, Hilary, Hesther, Hilda,
Rebecca, Sally, Mary, Imogen, Matilda,
Tracy, Taffetta, Bernadette,
Vivian, Olivia, Elaine, Yvette.

Eloisa, Artemisa, Jezebel, Joan,
Zsa-zsa, Nesta, Vesta, Pol, Simone,
Jo, Cloe, Zoe, Mo, Sheherezade,
Cleopatra, Clytemnestra, Hildegard.

Charlotte, Emily, Anne, Maria,
Emma, Gemma, Juliet, Penelope, Sophia,
Elsie, Ailsa, Agatha, Jane,
Vanessa, Farrers-Fawcett, Billie-Jean, Germain.

Celia, Amelia, Rosalind, Susannah,
Victoria, Elizabeth (*bow*) Diana,
Archbishop But in case your memory goes,
She'll be known to the world as Rose.

Here follows a verse, same tune, all singing the word "Rose". The Audience are conducted by Nurse and the Archbishop

King A right royal mouthful. There's no doubting she's a Princess now, eh.

Archbishop No, sire.

Nurse and the Queen are both fighting over the baby each trying to get it away from the Archbishop

Nurse She's mine
Queen She's mine.
Nurse It's my job to bring her up.
Queen It was my job getting her here in the first place.
Nurse All right. Just this once.
Archbishop The Fairy Godmothers. Where are the Fairy Godmothers?

The Godmothers come forward. Roxy has a piece of paper she's learning from

Godmothers (*together*) Here.
Queen You're sure you haven't asked—
King Yes! (*He is nervous, however*)
Nurse Why can't they have ordinary human godmothers?
Godmothers (*singing their jingle*)
        We have come to bless you
        With joys your whole life through,
        And Glynis here will make you rich
        Whatever you may do.
Glynis (*intoning*) Riches, riches be yours. (*She spreads a great deal of fairy dust over the baby which is in the Queen's arms, and waves her wand*)
Queen Oh isn't that nice. Isn't it really, Robert, riches.
King Yes. Hurry up.
Glynis It's your turn, Roxy.
Roxy You go, Blanche. I can't get my words right somehow.
Godmothers   Here is Blanche, whatever you may do.
        She will make you very wise
        Your whole life through.
Blanche (*intoning*) Wisdom, wisdom be yours. (*She sprinkles fairy dust and waves her wand*)
Queen Oh that was nice, too, wasn't it. Sort of spiritual.
King (*nervously*) Yes.
Glynis Come on, Roxy. Beauty. You'll spoil it if you don't go now.
Roxy Yeah, right then.
Godmothers   Here is Roxy ...

There is a sudden roar, like a jet aeroplane, and a great crash as one of the large crystal pieces shatters

    Maultash enters. She has on a black cloak and a horrible black hat and old tennis shoes. She is terrifying and coughs and spits and farts and is awful. If she doesn't fart she belches, or both, or something after these suggestions. She carries a broomstick

All Maultash! It's Maultash! Help! *Etc!*
Glynis Disaster, Blanche, disaster!
Blanche Don't be so hysterical.

Queen You said you hadn't asked her!

King I hadn't!

Maultash Why wasn't I invited to this affair?

Queen Because—because—Robert—(*She faints*)

Nurse (*rescuing the baby*) Wet. (*This refers to the Queen, not the baby*)

Maultash (*with a terrifying shout*) I said, why wasn't I invited to this affair?

Silence

King (*with sudden courage*) Because you're very, very nasty.

Maultash Yes. And I do some very nasty deeds. (*She gives a sudden "Sydney Greenstreet" sort of laugh*)

There is a flash of lightning and an explosion. Roxy runs and hides

Glynis Roxy, you're deserting us!

Roxy (*as she hides*) Shh!

Nurse I don't know who you are, but you shall not touch this child. It is a British Nursemaid who says this, and we are invincible.

Maultash belches

I'm not impressed.

Maultash (*referring to the baby*) Is that it?

Glynis Blanche, we must do something.

Blanche All right!

Glynis
Blanche (*together*) One, two, three, and—Maultash, be gone!

Maultash Oh, the Fairy Godmothers. Done your wingey little blessings, have you?

Glynis (*vibrato*) There was nothing wingey in them, they were wonderful! *Wonderful!*

Maultash And that means there's nothing you can do about mine when I give it. (*Mirthless laugh*)

Glynis Blanche, she's right! We can't go again, it's in the rules.

Blanche Sh!

King (*to the crowd*) Get at her. Go on, get at her.

Archbishop I'm afraid, actually we're too frightened.

Courtier Yes, we're too frightened.

Nurse You feeble, mardy bootses. She's only a witch.

Maultash (*indicating Nurse Hallowpenny*) You!

Nurse Now, don't you talk to me like ... (*She is suddenly paralysed*)

Maultash (*taking the baby*) Now, Princess—Misery, misery be yours! Before the end of your sixteenth birthday (*snigger*) just when you are at your prettiest (*snigger*) you will prick your finger on something sharp (*snigger*). And you will die! (*The snigger turns into hysterical laughter. She hands back the baby*)

Nurse Hallowpenny ceases being paralysed. There is thunder and flashes of lightning

King You beast. Get out! Go back to your awful cloud.

Maultash moves across to where the Queen lies and kicks her gently to wake her

Maultash Wake up! Your daughter's going to die before the end of her sixteenth birthday.

Queen Oh, Robert! (*She faints again*)

Maultash (*laughing*) So that's that! Oh, I do love christenings, I really do! (*She laughs and moves away*)

There is an explosion, a flash of lightning, a roar of aeroplane

Maultash has gone

King Cynthia? Cynthia!

Queen (*coming round*) Is it true, Robert?

King It's true and it's terrible.

Nurse There's no need to fear, Hallowpenny is here and I will keep Rose as safe as houses.

Glynis And we've failed, Blanche, we've failed.

Blanche Wait!

Roxy steps forward from her hiding place

Roxy Ahem! I haven't bestowed my blessing on this child yet. I cannot take away Maultash's spell because I'm only a very young fairy, but— (*twirl, twirl*)—I can make things much better.

Archbishop Oh, thank goodness for that because they're pretty bleak, I can tell you, they really are pretty bleak.

A kind of tinkling of Wagnerian leitmotif is heard from the pit

Roxy (*chanting*)   If the awful accident occurs
                                    And Rose should prick her finger as foretold
                                    She will not die, she'll fall asleep
                                    And stay so for one hundred years
                                    Until a prince arrives to kiss her into life.

(*She waves her wand*)

                                    Life, Life, I give you life!

All Life, Life, she gives her life!

Blanche You see, Glynis?

Glynis Oh Roxy, you make me so proud of you, sometimes.

Blanche It really was rather good.

Glynis But it didn't rhyme.

Roxy I think it sounds much better that way.

King That's wonderful! It really is wonderful! She's not going to die, Cynthia.

Queen Thank you so much, I can't tell you what it means.

Roxy I'm really really pleased you're pleased.

King ⎫
Queen ⎬ (*together, holding hands*) Oh, we are!

Nurse Nevertheless, if we can get her through her sixteenth birthday *without* pricking her finger—

King Champagne, everyone, lots of champagne.

Nurse I mean, after all, a hundred years is quite a long time to be asleep.

Queen The point is she won't die, Nurse Hallowpenny, so it's all right.

Nurse We should put a ban on all sharp pointed things and—

Queen Oh, stop spoiling everything and let's enjoy ourselves.

Nurse I'm not spoiling everything, I just think we should be sensible and not trust in magic the whole time. (*To Audience*) Really, this is so silly.

King To the Fairy Godmothers. Long may they look after us, and bless us.

Roxy Oh, we will, because we really, really enjoy it don't we, girls.

Glynis ⎱ (*together*) Yes.
Blanche ⎰

Glynis Oh, we do, we do. Tell them Roxy.

The Godmothers sing Song 8. This is a production number with dancing

Song 8: (She's got) Blue Eyes

Glynis   We're going to bless you
          With love your whole life through
          We'll make you happy
          Whatever you may do,
          Because of your Blue Eyes
          Because of your Baby Baby Blues

          Always in heaven
          Gazing down from above,
          We're everywhere, darling,
          To love and to love and to love you
          Because you've got
          Blue Eyes *etc*

          And we'll give you laughter
          To smile away the years,
          And when you need them
          Three shoulders for your tears,
          To dry your Blue Eyes *etc*.

Chorus   Because she's got Blue Eyes,
          Baby's got those Baby Baby Blue Eyes
          Baby's got those Baby Baby Blue Eyes
          All because of your Baby Baby Blues

Blanche Better now?

Glynis Oh, much!

Roxy Lovely. Let's leave them to muddle through for a bit, then.

The Godmothers leave

Nurse (*stepping forward*) All right, all right, all right. But magic or no magic, from now on it will be my duty to see that Rose has absolutely nothing sharp anywhere near her at all.

King Nurse Hallowpenny ...

Nurse I don't want any Royal bleating from you. Where are those two eager beavers who are so very helpful if you whip them along?

1 and 2 come in pushing a large cast iron hideosity of a thing which has an opening at the top and a notice saying "Sharpness Disposal Unit"

1
2 } (*together*) Here, Nurse Hallowpenny. At once, Nurse Hallowpenny.

1 There we are. A Sharpness Disposal Unit.

All A Sharpness Disposal Unit!

Nurse Good. From now on, these two gentlemen have been appointed Point Inspectors to the Royal Family.

King Who by?

Nurse You.

King Oh good.

Queen Robert?

King Well, it is quite a good idea.

Nurse It's a very good idea and well done, King Robert.

King Point Inspectors, how does this Sharpness Disposal Unit work?

1 Like this, Your Majesty. Attend.

1 topples the King's crown into the Unit and sounds like a large shredder, grinding and roaring, are heard

King My crown!

Nurse We can't have little Rose pricking herself on a crown. (*She takes the Queen's Crown*)

Queen Oh! That's mine.

King We must all make sacrifices. What else can we put in?

The Audience are involved in shouting things out. Here is a useful list of things that are put in:

Pins, needles, knives, forks, brooches, pens, pencils, razors, scissors, nails, screws, garden forks, hedge clippers, broken glass and crystal pointed knobs on the throne

The King loses a brooch holding on his cloak, a tie pin holding a cravat, a safety pin holding up his breeches, and his pointed shoes

Each loss is accompanied by the company saying the phrase "For the good of the Princess"

Ad lib, then, ominously, a skipping rope is put in

Queen Oh, but surely—

2 She might fall over and cut herself.

Nurse Quite right. All games.

In go the skipping rope, and other things such as darts, perhaps some of these are associated with the Band or the Archbishop

(*When all is complete*) There we are. Safe.
1 Safe.
2 Safe.
King
Queen } (*together*) I suppose so.
Nurse Off you go. Now keep your eyes peeled for points. Points everyone, points!

There is a general exodus

Courtier The next sixteen years are going to be absolutely miserable.

Black-out

SCENE 5

Front cloth

The Godmothers enter

Glynis We can't wait sixteen years to see what happens. People will get hungry.
Blanche We can make time pass, Glynis, as you know very well. Roxy, the clock. Now then. Ask the children to help make time pass quickly.

A large clock descends from the flies

A round is started. The Fairy Godmothers persuade the children to start singing it

Song 9: Tick Tock Round

Godmothers   Tick, tock, tick, tock,
                        Time is passing round the clock,
                        Days and nights and weeks and years,
                        Time is never still.

Finally, the clock stops at sixteen and goes off like an alarm

Glynis We've done it. Well done!

The Godmothers exit

Black-out

SCENE 6

The Palace Gardens. The day before the sixteenth birthday

The garden is beautiful, with vistas of open countryside, but also has walls

  Nurse Hallowpenny enters with Crispin, now a practical young man of sixteen

Nurse Sixteen long years have passed, then, and I'm still here guarding Rose with my life. There's just tomorrow to get through and then I'll have more time to look for my own true love. In the meantime, Just look at this. (*She demonstrates Crispin*) Crispin of the Cardboard Box, this is. Reared him with my own hands, and proud of him, oh, am I proud of him. He's practical, he's trustworthy, he's good at sports, he can sew, he's going to learn to read—I could hug him.

Crispin Just tell them about tomorrow, Hallowpenny.

Nurse He might be my own, you know. He's such a *good* boy.

Crispin Hallowpenny! Please.

Nurse Well, tomorrow is Rose's sixteenth birthday, and the security precautions in the castle are terrific. There isn't a point anywhere. And Rose—oh Rose has grown into such a—a ...

Crispin Thoroughly wonderful girl. Rose, come on out here.

Rose (*off*) Oh, I can come in the garden, can I?

Nurse Now don't get in a mood, madam, please.

  Rose enters, a beautiful and spirited girl

Rose I'm absolutely sick to death of being cooped up in this ridiculous palace with no friends, no fun, no food but sandwiches, no knives and no forks, no comb for my hair, no ear-rings, no brooches, no bows and arrows, no pens, no pencils—I'm bored, bored, bored!

Crispin Poor Rose, but there's only one more day, isn't there.

Rose Poor Rose, poor Rose, that's all anyone ever says.

Nurse (*seeing a thistle*) Stand still! A thistle! Point Inspectors! I thought you'd checked this garden!

  1 and 2 rush in saying "sorry, Nurse Hallowpenny" etc, and carrying several pieces of equipment

  1 and 2 rush about with their equipment

1 and 2 Thistle exterminator? Here. Prickle container? Here. Where's the briar blunter? Here. (*They busy over this*)

Rose Can I see?

Nurse Of course not.

Rose It should be part of my education.

Crispin If she's never seen a thistle, how will she know how to avoid one?

Nurse I simply can't risk it. There may be loose thorns flying all over the place.

1 and 2 One, two, three, heave.

The thistle is out

Off to the Sharpness Disposal Unit with it. There, right.

1 and 2 exit with the thistle and their equipment

Rose Honestly. And all because of some silly story about falling asleep for a hundred years.

Nurse (*to the Audience*) But it's true, isn't it, children?

Audience Yes.

Nurse I keep telling her, but she's so self-willed, keeps trying to escape, going behind my back, playing tricks, making plots—keep away from the flowers.

Rose Oh, Hallowpenny, what harm is there in flowers?

Nurse Well, you never know there could be a bee lurking in there, or a wasp. Or a hornet.

Crispin Hallowpenny, I think you've been overdoing it. You'd better leave her with me, and have a rest.

Nurse All right. I trust you, Crispin. (*To the Audience*) They employ him in the saddleroom, you know. Wonderful horseman, wonderful. (*Speaking off as she starts to exit*) File down the gravel on the front drive, you lot, and get moving.

Nurse Hallowpenny exits

Rose It's been the same all my life. One long panic. (*Gazing at the distant countryside*) I'd love to get out there. Look at those daisies growing so wild!

Crispin You'll be able to the day after tomorrow. You'll even be able to play games.

Rose Games! Hallowpenny stops me playing games in case I fall and cut myself, so I'm going to look a real fool when I first go out of the palace gate, aren't I. A really big fool.

Crispin (*looking round*) Well—look—I don't suppose it would hurt if I taught you how to play something gentle, would it, like Grandmother's Footsteps.

Rose Oh, Crispin, yes.

Crispin Well, what you do is . . .

1 and 2 and the Archbishop appear

1 Ah ah! I'm afraid the Princess may not play games until after—

Rose Spies! Always spies!

2 It isn't us, it's Hallowpenny!

Rose You can jolly well come and join in. I command you.

1 It will end in tears, I know.

2 Oh, come on. It's just this once.

Archbishop I haven't had a good game of Grandmother's Footsteps in years.

Rose Show us, Crispin.

Crispin You stand there, Rose, and we creep up. We have to be still or we're out.

Crispin gives an ad lib explanation of the game's rules, then they have a trial run with much laughter, then on to the song

Song 10: Grandmother's Footsteps

All   Grandmother's footsteps,
                  One, two, three.
                  Turn around and you can see
                  Who's been moving, he or she—
                  To the back in Grandmother's footsteps.

Rose fails to turn

2 You'd better explain again, Crispin, she doesn't understand.

Crispin explains again. They are about to start, then:

We really need some more people. Let's get some.

Some of the children from the Audience are invited on to the stage to join in the game. When the game is going well and one of the children is grand-mother—

Nurse Hallowpenny enters

Nurse Crispin! What on earth is this!
Crispin Nothing, Hallowpenny. (*He smuggles the children offstage*)
Nurse It's Grandmother's Footsteps, that's what it is. And you allowed it Crispin, you whom I've always trusted. You put Rose's life in danger at this last moment. Suppose she'd fallen over?
Crispin I wouldn't have let that happen, Hallowpenny.
Nurse You all say that, don't you, but how could you have stopped it? I raised you from a cardboard box to be the playmate of a princess, and this is how you repay me, all of you. (*To the Audience*) Even you. I thought you children were sensible, and even you have let me down, joining in, singing and that. I'm very very hurt. My Rose, my little Rose. Come with me and be safe.

Nurse leads Rose off

Rose (*calling as she goes*) It was lovely learning that game. Thank you. I shall never forget it, ever.
Archbishop No wonder she never finds her own true love.
2 Be like marrying a grapefruit.
1 Right, no more hanky panky. Anyone with birthday presents for the Princess Rose, please bring them to the check point for point checking.
2 Oh! You're getting witty as well as helpful.

1 and 2 exit

Archbishop Jumped up civil servants.

The Archbishop exits

Crispin (*To the Audience*) Only one more day and then Rose will be free of the witch's spell. I wonder how she really feels about it?

Black-out

SCENE 7

What the Princess Thinks

Rose is seen in a spotlight

Song 11: To Be Me

Rose (*singing*)

I want to be
Wild as the sea.
I want to be
Rough as the waves
Tumble and turn with the tide
And be nobody's slave.
'Cos I'd rather be me.

I want to be
Swimming in light.
I want to be
Bright as the sun,
Silent and pale as the moon
When the dark night has come,
And I long to be me

ME—Talking to strangers.
ME—Opening doors.
ME—a babe in a manger no more.
I want to be
Strong as the storm.
I want to be
Soft as the snow,
Bite like the ice in the wind,
Yet be always aglow

And I want to know
Love and adventure.
I want to let go of my heart.
Give me my life
And I'll take it again from the start.
If I could only be me.

ME—Breathless with wonder
ME—Under the sky
ME—Finally learning to fly!

> If I could only be me.
> Let me be me.

Repeat

Black-out at end of song

SCENE 8

The Sixteenth Birthday

A court yard; or another part of the garden

There is bunting and banners saying "happy birthday" and there is a tower set a little behind into which we will see in time

In the foreground is a table or box with Rose's present on it or in it. It is one hanky

The court is assembled, but everyone looks very grim. Hallowpenny is grim-faced and tense. Rose is furious. Crispin is sad for her. The King and Queen look very nervous about the whole thing

1 and 2 play the trumpets. This time the sound is so beautiful and loud the two men are amazed

Rose (*holding up the hanky*) Is this the only birthday present I've got?
Nurse The others were hopelessly dangerous. That's from me.
Queen What about the mirror I gave her?
Nurse Suppose it broke? There'd be bits of pointed glass all over the place.
King What happens now?
Nurse Nothing. Rose has to be guarded closely the whole day.
Queen I'd like to have a little talk with her in private, actually. I haven't had one in sixteen years.
Nurse She needs to be guarded by someone competent.
Queen I'm competent. Tell her, Robert.
Nurse You've never been competent, that's the whole trouble—insisting on Fairy Godmothers.

The Queen howls

Well it's true.
King Nurse Hallowpenny, that is the Queen.
Nurse And you're just as bad. Always taking the easy way out!
King Oh, I say, come on—
Nurse I'm sorry, I'm sorry, I'm sorry. I'm all strung up and worried, that's all.
Rose And you're making this the horridest day of my life.
Nurse It's for your own good.
Rose As usual.

There is silence

King Are we really going to spend all day here doing nothing, then?

Nurse Yes.

Rose You're absolutely the most horrible person I can remember.

Nurse I'm not! I'm the sort of person who is usually full of joy and happiness!

Rose I've never seen it!

King Nor me.

Queen Nor me.

Others murmur the same

Nurse I'm cross and awkward because I don't want her to fall asleep for a hundred years, that's all. It's because I love her.

All (*variously*) Huh.

Crispin It is true, Your Majesty. I know Hallowpenny better than any of you do and she's really a very dashing old sport.

Nurse Old?

Crispin Hallowpenny, if we all promise not to take Rose away from here will you show us—you know—that thing you used to do?

Nurse What, you mean?—(*she mimes a hand jive*)

Crispin Yes.

Nurse Oh, I couldn't possibly. No.

All Oh, yes, promise.

Crispin Oh, please, Nurse Hallowpenny. After all it is Rose's birthday, and she didn't get any proper presents, so she deserves something nice.

Nurse We—ll. Ooh, you know how to get round me, Crispin, don't you. Well I suppose if it'll make them understand me a bit better and love me a little. Here goes then.

Song 12: The Gutbuster

Nurse sings the Introduction very demurely before launching into the rip-roaring Song—which should come as a shock to all

Introduction   When I was a student nanny
                   People were appalled
                   I used to cut a caper
                   To a two-step that was called

Song   THE GUTBUSTER THE GUTBUSTER
                   You lift it, shift it,
                   And glitter with lustre
                   A rompin' stompin'
                   Hoofin' snap of a dance step.

                   You root toot it and zoot suit it,
                   And stamp your feet to the beat
                   That's so cute it'll
                   Make you shut your eyes
                   And float to a trance step.

	There's rhythm shaking
	Your bones and making
Sung twice	A zylophone out of your spine.
	It joins the pull of
	Your toes so full of
	The twitching itch to climb cloud nine.

So get groovin' it.
Keep movin' it,
Life's a ball and you could be
Provin' it,
Spread the joy of dancing over the nation

Dance

Do The Gutsbuster,
The Gutbuster,
You lift it, shift it,
And glitter with lustre
A rompin', stompin' hoofin' snap of a—
Thumpin', jumpin', happy tap of a—
Swingin', ringin' flyin' fling of a
Dance step.

Queen That *was* fun. Now I'm going to have my little talk with my daughter.

Nurse No! You promised you wouldn't go!

Crispin (*to the Queen*) You did.

Queen That was before we realized Nurse Hallowpenny was just like the rest of us.

All Yes, yes, just like us.

Nurse If you're going, I must come too.

Queen Stop her, Robert. I want to be alone with Rose.

Rose (*excited, or flushed, by the dance*) Mother, you can talk to me later. Dont's upset Nurse Hallowpenny when she's all happy.

Queen Is that what she is?

Nurse Oh ... Queens. I'm up to here with them.

King Can't you teach us all some more of those giddy steps to pass the time, Hallowpenny?

Rose Oh yes, do. You'll love that, won't you mother?

Queen Well, if you promise I can have my talk with you later ...

Rose Yes, yes, you show us, Hallowpenny. Keep us all occupied.

Nurse Well, there was this provocative little routine we used to work up to after the third cup of cocoa.

Everybody becomes involved in learning the dance and following Nurse Hallowpenny. Rose backs away

Crispin (*joining Rose*) Rose, where are you going?

Rose Crispin, will you get me a bunch of those daisies we saw yesterday?

Crispin I can't leave you.

Rose But I haven't had any flowers for my birthday, and daisies are quite safe, with no points on them. Please, Crispin? Some flowers?

Crispin Well ... don't move, will you?

Rose Of course not.

Crispin Then I'll go.

Crispin exits

Rose (*to the Audience*) Alone. I'm alone, for the first time in sixteen years. It's marvellous!

The tower moves forward and Rose moves somehow to come near it. the interior of the tower is lit up and Maultash can be seen inside with a spinning wheel

Oh, the tower. And look, a little staircase in the tower that I've never seen before.

Rose goes in and up and comes to the little room where Maultash can be seen sitting spinning

Hello. Is that a spinning wheel?

Maultash Have you never seen one?

Rose No.

Maultash Then come in my dear, and try it.

Rose (*with a radiant smile*) Oh, thank you.

Maultash How pretty you look my love.

Rose Do I? What a clumsy thing a spinning wheel is to use.

Maultash Not if you're careful.

Rose (*indicating the distaff*) Do I hold this in my hands like this?

Maultash Yes.

Rose And then move it like this.

Maultash Yes.

Rose And then—Oh! I've pricked my thumb! (*Then, with pain*) Ow. Oh. Hallowpenny! (*She rushes down the stairs*) Hallowpenny. I've pricked my thumb! On a spinning wheel.

Rose is now back with the Court

Queen Rose?

Maultash (*from the tower*) You stupid parents! She's dying. Your daughter's dying.

The lights in the tower go out

Nurse Who let her go?

Queen You did.

Nurse You did.

With a sigh, Rose, who has been swaying, sinks to the ground beautifully

(*On her knees*) Rose! Oh my darling Rose!

Queen (*clutching the King*) Oh, Robert!

Nurse (*holding Rose*) I should never have taken my eyes off her.

King Where are those point inspectors?
1 and 2 Er—
King You should've stopped that spinning wheel from getting there. Leave this palace and never come back again.
1 and 2 Yes, Your Majesty. Of course, Your Majesty. Let's get back to the foyer, then.

1 and 2 exit

King If only I'd been stronger and more sensible about the whole business!
Queen No, it's my fault.
Nurse No, it's my fault.

They compete for the blame

The Godmothers enter

Blanche Now, now, now, now, now, now. Stop all this fuss, because she's only asleep for a hundred years, that's all.
Roxy You hear, Maultash? She's only asleep for a hundred years, and then a prince will come and wake her with a kiss.
Maultash (*unseen in the darkened tower*) A what?
Roxy A kiss.
Maultash Ah, you wretched little wimp of a do-gooder. No prince is going to reach her. I'll make a forest grow round her too thick for anyone to penetrate. Just you wait.

There is a great peal of evil laughter from Maultash. The roaring of her broomstick is heard as she "takes off" and her laughter dies away

Glynis Oh, I hate magic forests. She is the end.
Roxy (*when peace is restored*) Come what may, I know a prince will come and find her.
Archbishop My goodness, I hope so.
King But what about us? Are we going to stay here and starve to death?
Glynis Yes, you will, you will!
Blanche Oh no. You will go to sleep like Rose, so when she wakes up you'll be there to help her.
King You mean—
Queen But surely—
Nurse I don't want to go—
Archbishop Well, I suppose—

And they are asleep—snoring gently

Roxy Aahh! How sweet, Blanche.
Glynis Oh, Blanche, you're so clever.
Blanche You must learn to take things easy, dear.

Glynis and Blanche go

Glynis (*as she goes*) I'll try.

Crispin enters with a bunch of daisies

Crispin Rose. Rose?

Roxy Too late, love. You'd better come and have an ice-cream while I tell
you what's happened.

Roxy leads Crispin off, sadly

The Lights change to night. Owls hoot and a voice comes over the speakers

Voice There will now be an interval of one hundred years.

C<small>URTAIN</small>

ENTR'ACTE

A Frontcloth

1 and 2 appear on stage with an Eastern Prince—played by the actor who was Crispin in the first act

1 (*to the orchestra*) Stop. Stop that noise. A Royal person has come to see the second act. House Lights out, follow spot, please.

2 A roll of drums, please.

1 The National Anthem of Hindinapplestan.

2 Makes His Royal Highness feel comfy if we sing his song.

The drum roll starts

1
2 } (*together*) Stand please, everyone, stand please.

Prince Stop! Stop, please stop!

The drum roll ceases

And sit down, everyone. I'm not that sort of prince at all. I don't like people standing up for me.

1 You—Don't be silly. All princes like people standing up for them.

Prince Well, I don't. I'm so sorry.

1 But you have to.

2 We know, we've worked with royalty.

1 Kings, queens, princesses, we know all about them. They like people standing up for them.

2 You clearly need us to put you right about a thing or two, or you'll get nowhere in the prince business.

1 You leave everything to us, and we'll have you in the Top Drawer before you can say knife. Right?

2 Right.

1 and 2 ad lib with each other as they persuade the Prince to go into a box, preferably right on the side of the stage

Prince (*as he is persuaded into the box*) Well, I don't wish any National Anthem.

1 Very well, just this once. (*To 2*) We're on to a good thing here.

2 He'll take us back to the Royal Palace.

1 Put us up at the Ritz.

2 Days out on the Royal Yacht

1 and 2 chuckle together

1 (*as the Prince reaches the box*) Ah, there you are, Prince! Sit back in your seat. Look a bit foolish, a bit stuffy—

2 That's it. And don't get involved with anything that goes on up here.

1 It always goes wrong if you do.

2 As we know to our cost (*He begins to leave*) Just enjoy the show.

There is a sudden loud shriek-cum-moan off-stage

Prince (*leaping to his feet*) What's that?

2 It's all right. It's just one of the fairy godmothers. Sit down. (*He tries again to leave*) Don't want him getting caught in anything back there.

1 No.

Glynis (*off*) Oh woe, woe, misery and despair!

Prince (*to 1*) Can I help?

1 No! Just sit back and enjoy yourself. Look a bit more foolish, will you, less enthusiastic.

> *1 and 2 exit*

The moaning off stage continues

> *Blanche and Roxy enter*

Roxy (*to the Audience*) It's Glynis. She's gone right over the top. Really really over hedgerows.

Blanche We are slightly worried about things, actually, but there's no need to go this far. Look at her.

Glynis enters with her "Luccia di Lammermoor" look

Song 13: We Need a Royal Personage—Oh

Glynis (*singing*) The hundred years have passed away at last.
　　　　　　　We need a prince to come and do his duty.
　　　　　　　But none appears, and I am much downcast,
　　　　　　　For if we fail, we lose our sleeping beauty.

Blanche (*speaking; aside*) The last century has been an awful strain on her.

Prince (*speaking; aside*) I'm a prince.

1 and 2 pop on again

1
2 } (*together, to the Prince*) Ssh! Ssh!

Glynis (*singing*) We cannot cheat, the spell must go its way.
　　　　　　　We can't pretend a commoner is regal,
　　　　　　　So if you know where princes romp and play,
　　　　　　　Then nick one for us, though it proves illegal.

Prince (*speaking*) I'm a prince.

1
2 } (*together, speaking*) Stay where you are, sire. Don't get involved.

All Godmothers (*singing*) We need a royal personage—oh
　　　　　　　　　　Handsome, brave or simply cosy.
　　　　　　　　　　We'd take one of almost any age—oh
　　　　　　　　　　So long as he will kiss our Rosie.
　　　　　　　　　　The time has come for all to wake—oh
　　　　　　　　　　And greet the morning so romantic
　　　　　　　　　　So wearing helmet, crown, or shakoh,
　　　　　　　　　　For princes we are simply frantic.

Meanwhile, the Prince has begun to climb out of the box by means of a ladder of some sort, and 1 and 2 are trying to stop him

Prince (*singing*) I'm a prince,
I'm very loyal,
Quite gallant
And pretty royal.
Give me a chance,
I'll do whatever
You may require
With great endeavour.
I'm a prince

Meanwhile, dashing between the Godmothers who they want to be rid of, and the Prince whom they want to stay seated, 1 and 2 sing as follows

1
2 } (*together*) Play something different.
Now be your age
Sit and eat ice cream,
Please leave the stage,
Don't leave the box sire,
Give it a miss.
Nothing but trouble
Will come from all this.

Harmonizing

1 and 2
Godmothers } (*together*)

Play something different. **Prince** A Royal Prince,
Now be your age   A loyal Prince,
Sit and eat ice cream.   I'm gallant.
Please leave the stage.   Quite talented too
Don't leave the box sire,   And my blood is blue.
Give it a miss.   I'm telling you
Nothing but trouble   What you see when you see me's
Will come from all this.   A genuine Royal Prince

Harmonizing

Prince I'm telling you that I'——m
Godmothers   What we're looking for's
1 and 2   What we need's a pro—

Prince
Godmothers } (*together*) A prince
1 and 2   A prince
                               —per Prince

At the end of the song the Prince has managed to climb onto the stage

Prince Ladies, I am a prince so can I help you?
Blanche Oh Glynis, pull yourself together.
Roxy I think he's here. In fact, I'm sure he is.

Glynis That's not a prince.
Roxy Well it could be, actually.
Blanche Yes, it could be.
1 Well, not really.
2 He's a sort of a prince, but he's not the sort you're looking for.
Prince I might be.
1 Oh no, because they're looking for the sort of prince who's going to get involved with a lot of awful things back there. So sorry. Sorry, he's not what you want, he's ours.

1 and 2 begin to pull the Prince away

Glynis He looks like someone we know.
Roxy (*innocently*) Does he?
Prince (*breaking away*) But I want to help them.
1 Look. As a proper prince, you've got to be good at the sneering. How's your sneering eh?
2 Rotten. This is a sneer, this (*he demonstrates a sneer*) See, you can't do it. Sorry, sorry, he's not what you want.
Blanche Sneering isn't important.
2 Ah, but the waving. He's a very bad waver, aren't you? There. That's a good-bye wave, not a royal wave. The children can do better than that. (*He ad libs objections*)
1 See, this is the wave. A little titchy flick of the finger nails. No, you see, no good.
1 ⎫
2 ⎭ (*together*) Sorry, sorry, sorry, so sorry.

Blanche Just one minute, please.
1 Have you seen his salute, then? His salute?
2 He's no good at the salute, are you? No.
1 Nor inspecting the troops, like this.
2 Nor shaking hands with Lords and Ladies.
1 Nor grinning.
2 Nor laughing.
1 Nor looking serious.
2 Nor giving people medals.
1 Nor chopping off their heads.
Both Sorry. Back to your box, eat your ice cream, don't get involved. Wrong chap altogether.
Prince They won't want me to chop off people's heads.
1 Ah, now, won't they.
Godmothers No.
Blanche What's his name?
Prince Claude.
Godmothers (*surprised and disappointed*) Claude?
1 ⎫
2 ⎭ (*together*) You see?

Claude Prince Claude of Hindinapplestan.
Blanche Hindinapplestan?

1 Too silly.

Roxy It's not.

Glynis Princes aren't usually called Claude. Blanche, they aren't.

1
2 } (*together*) They never are. So sorry, sorry, sorry—

Prince If it helps to prove that I'm a prince, I keep having this dream about a sleeping castle.

Godmothers What?

1
2 } (*together*) Oh, Lord.

Prince And there's a King in it and a Queen in it, and a Princess who seems to have hurt her thumb.

Blanche Roxy, this could be it.

Glynis Who else is there?

Prince A strange and mysterious lady called—Halfpenny? Halliwell? Hallowpenny!

Blanche It's him!

Glynis Yippee! It is him! Oh boy, oh boy!

Roxy A real, real, real live prince, I told you.

1
2 } (*together*) Oh Lord, oh Lord!

Song 14: Sleeping Beauty's Boy

Godmothers (*singing*) Oh here's the prince
Who'll never wince
A lovely boy, we've got him!
Though middle class
He's bold as brass
Oh clever us
To spot him!

He's going to Rose
And heaven knows
A man so strong and active
Will win the day
And anyway,
He's terribly attractive.

Chorus

Oh-ho
Hi-ho
Through the forest he will go
Hoi polloi
And full of joy
He's the Sleeping Beauty's Boy.

1
2 } (*together*)   He's nothing much
                      To speak of, such
                      A midget he needs feeding.
                      And at the least
                      He's not a feast
                      Of manners and good breeding.
                      If he's so good
                      We think you should
                      Expect some more to go on
                      To show he can
                      Prove he's the man
                      To win the girl and so on.

Chorus

                      Oh-ho
                      Hi-ho
                      Through the forest? Dear me no.
                      Hoi polloi
                      Not much joy
                      He's not the Sleeping Beauty's Boy.

Prince   I can't agree
                      When you make me
                      Sound absolutely zero
                      Though modest, I
                      Have to reply
                      I could turn out the hero.

                      I have this dream
                      In which I seem
                      To see the girl I long for
                      The one for me
                      I want to be
                      So big and brave and strong for

Chorus

                      Oh-ho
                      Hi-ho
                      Through the forest love will go
                      Hoi polloi
                      Full of joy
                      I am the Sleeping Beau——ty's   Boy

Godmothers   Oh, yes he is; he's the boy.
1 and 2   Oh no he's not; oh, no he's not the boy

Prince (*speaking*) And I'll make a dream come on now and prove it to you.

Dream music is heard as the Prince goes into a trance

The CURTAIN rises on

ACT II

Scene 1

The Dream of the Palace

We are in the Courtyard where the Court fell asleep. A gauze could be used here, so the scene "shimmers". The sleeping bodies of the King, the Queen, Nurse Hallowpenny, the Archbishop and Rose can be seen, lying as we last saw them. They are, in fact, life-like dummies of the actors, so that the real persons can "step out" from their "bodies" to enact Prince Claude's dream

Slowly, leaving his body behind, the dream of the King gets up

King (*to the Audience*) Here we are again. Someone's dreaming us. It makes a change from the eternal snooze.

Queen (*leaving her "body"*) Someone dreaming us again, Robert?

King (*peering out front*) Yes, dear.

Queen (*peering out front*) Same person?

King I can't quite tell, but I should think so.

Rose (*waking*) Daddy? Is it wake up time?

King No dear. I'm afraid it's just another dream.

Rose Oh, if only I hadn't pricked my thumb. If only—if only—if only!

Nurse (*waking*) Oh! Woe! Misery!

King Oh Lord!

Queen Oh, do be quiet, Hallowpenny.

Nurse It's all my fault! If only I'd let you have a bit more freedom none of this would've happened.

Rose You could say if only I'd been a bit more careful.

Nurse No, it's my fault.

Rose No it's my fault.

Nurse No, it's *MY* fault!

King Everytime someone dreams us, you go blubbing on about it all being your fault.

Queen You just made a mistake, that's all. Everyone makes mistakes.

Nurse Not me. I never make mistakes! I did something wicked—I danced—and I'm being punished for it, and I'm terribly unhappy, and I like being unhappy, and nothing you can do can stop it, so don't try, because I'm going to go on moaning and groaning for ever and ever, amen, and even longer than that, and what's more you'll be sorry when I'm dead.

Queen Oh dry up, Betty. You look far too nice in your dream outfit for all this.

Rose Betty? Oh! Betty! Ha ha!

Nurse Rose! Why don't you drop off again. You're the Sleeping Beauty, please remember. (*To the Queen*) Who said you could call me Betty?

Queen We're being dreamed, enjoy it.

Nurse Don't try to cheer me up, Cynthia.

King Who are you calling Cynthia.

Nurse Well, it's only a dream, isn't it. (*She gives a little laugh*).

King So long as it's only a dream, you can call me Bobby, if you want to.

Queen No, she can't.

King Why not?

Queen Because you're the King. *My* King. And we must concentrate on this person who keeps dreaming us.

Rose I wonder who it can be?

Nurse It's probably my own true love.

King Oh, honestly.

Nurse Well, it could be.

King Sh.

The Archbishop snores

   Who's doing that?

Roxy The Archbishop.

Nurse What a peaceful sight it is.

The Archbishop snores again

Nurse Turn over, your Grace, there's a dear.

Queen Something's upsetting me. What is it? (*She wriggles, and turns to look at her body*)

Queen Aaah! It's a spider. It's crawling over me. Look!

Nurse Aha! I'll deal with that. Out you eight legged boss-eyed lump of fat. Stop crawling over the Queen.

Roxy Let me help.

Rose and Nurse Hallowpenny beat away at it, and the blows are felt by the dream Queen. The spider evidently gets to the King's "body"

   Where've you gone? Come on, let's have you.

Nurse Oh, the devil! It's on the King!

The King wriggles and then is "hit" as above

   Now where are you. Oh, on me. (*after much care, she wallops the Nurse Hallowpenny "body" very hard on the head. This causes her to stagger widely*)

Rose Oh, Hallowpenny, Hallowpenny, are you all right?

Nurse Yes, of course I am.

King So who doesn't make mistakes? Who's an old clever, clever?

Rose There now, Hallowpenny.

Nurse (*severely*) Just concentrate on this—Bobby. Is it my own true love, or isn't it?

Queen Who on earth would choose to dream you up when there was me?

Nurse May I point out that someone is dreaming me up at this very moment.

Queen They're dreaming me up as well, and if you don't mind my saying so, if—

Nurse
Queen } (*together*) They're dreaming you up, it must be a nightmare!

King For heavens sake, quiet! Someone is dreaming us because they want to know something about us.

Nurse They're dreaming us because some of us are fascinating.

Queen You're right, Robert. They want to be told—to be told—Is it the way to reach us?

Rose Aha! It's one of those recognition dreams.

King What are they?

Rose Well, someone dreams a dream and then tells someone and they say "Oh, well if you're dreaming that, you must be so and so".

Nurse Nurse Hallowpenny's own true love, for example.

The Archbishop gives a snorting snore

King Oh, do turn over for heaven's sake ... I mean, you know.

Queen It's not your own true love, Hallowpenny. It's the prince who's going to wake us up.

Nurse It could be.

King I think it is.

Rose I'm not marrying him just because he wakes me up, you know.

Nurse Well, don't say it too loudly. He might hear.

King Cooee! We're waiting.

Queen Hurry, please.

Nurse Come on. We're the dream you want! Come and get us.

Rose Yes, come and wake us up anyway! We'll see about the rest afterwards.

Song 15: Dream of a Dream

All (*singing*)   We're just the dream of a dream,
Of dreams you could dream
We're the cream of the cream,
And we are waiting for you
To make our dreams come true.

We're here inside your head,
Snoozing the years away
Tucked up in bed.
Plenty of nothing to do
Waiting to be woken by you
And then our dream'll come true.

We've been pretty deep
In this magical sleep,
We're feeling as cold as the clay,
But we think you'll find
When we're outside your mind
And into the world again we'll be OK.

    For we're just the dreamiest bunch,
    Keeping our spirits alive
    With the hunch
    That one day you'll know what to do
    To make our dream come true.

    Repeat the previous two verses

    That one day you'll know what to do
    To give us back the life that we knew
    On the outside of you,
    To make our dreams come true,
    Please make our dream come true

Everyone goes back into their "bodies" to continue the long sleep

SCENE 2

Back to the front cloth. Only 1 and 2 are on the stage

1 Prince, where are you?

2 Where are you, Prince?

Prince (*off*) Good-bye. I'm going to rescue the Sleeping Beauty.

1 (*crossly*) He's gone back there.

2 (*crossly*) Got involved with his dream.

1
2 } (*together*) We've lost him.

1 Drat.

2 Bother.

1 Well—*he* won't come to any good.

2 Oh no. It never pays to go around being brave all over the place.

1 Show off. (*To the Audience*) You pay attention, so you don't make the same mistake that he did. (*To the Orchestra*) Thank you.

Song 16: Don't Be Brave

1 and 2 If you want to lead a cosy, warm existence,
(*singing*) Then avoid the whiff of risk, the smell of strife.
    Why awake the Sleeping Beauty
    When she could turn awfully snooty?
    There are plainer girls who'd make a better wife.

    If the Godmothers call out for your assistance,
    To save the Royal Family, don't be rash.
    Do not move or make suggestions
    Till they've answered all your questions—
    Is it easy? Is it safe? And where's the cash?

Chorus

> Don't be brave
> That's the rule
> Where the angels fear to tread, don't be a fool.
> If you ever think you might
> Become a faintly shining knight,
> Then ignore the maiden's wave,
> Don't be brave.
>
> Seven dwarfs have seen you lonely and unhappy,
> And they ask you in to cook for them forthwith,
> Say, "I'm sorry, I'm not stopping",
> Or you'll end up with the shopping,
> Cleaning, washing AND a poisoned Granny Smith.
>
> Or you're trotting through the country on your charger,
> When a king runs up and offers you a bride.
> "All you have to do is slaughter
> One old dragon for me daughter" —
> Will you make much of a husband when you're fried?

Repeat Chorus

> Don't offer help to girls called Cinderella —
> You'll be turned into a pumpkin like as not.
> Do not stoop to kiss a froggy
> Who's slimey, fat and soggy —
> If he stays like that, you're really in a spot.
>
> When you wake to find a beanstalk in your garden,
> And your mother's got this idea in her head,
> She says "I've got this hunch"
> Why don't you climb it after lunch?"
> Just say "On yer bike" and send her up instead!

Repeat Chorus

> ... faintly shining knight
> If a quiet life you crave
> And your precious skin you'd save,
> Then avoid an early grave
> And don't be brave ...!

1 and 2 exit, running

The sound of wind and thunder takes us to—

SCENE 3

Maultash's Awful Cloud. It is windy and thundery

The Cloud can be on a truck. 1 and 2 enter, running, but are stopped in their tracks by magic from Maultash's broomstick, from afar

Maultash You snivelling saveloys! You greasy chip papers you. (*As a great howl*) You gave them a prince!

1
2 } (*together*) We didn't! We tried to keep him for ourselves. We did everything we could to stop him. We told him not to get caught up in the story.

Maultash Like you are. (*chuckling*) Welcome to the Awful Cloud.

1 Great.

2 Lovely.

Maultash Are you comfortable?

1
2 } (*together*) Not exactly. No, actually, not.

Maultash points her broomstick which screws them up worse. They scream. She laughs and then relaxes slightly

Maultash Better?

1
2 } (*together*) Much.

Maultash turns them around by magic to face her

Maultash Ask me why I brought you here.

1
2 } (*together*) Why did you—

Maultash Because I need some helpful people at the moment, and you go in for that sort of thing, don't you?

1
2 } (*together*) Oh yes, frightfully, awfully, couldn't be more.

Maultash Well then, this prince of yours has to go.

1
2 } (*together*) Go?

Maultash Go. I've grown my rose forest round the castle—

1 Nice one. That'll beat him. A rose forest. Wow! Good thinking.

Maultash But with a decent sword he looks the sort of horribly determined young man who might cut through it.

2 Someone like you shouldn't be put off by something as trivial as that.

Maultash We're not allowed to cheat, you know. Once a spell has been put on, we aren't allowed to meddle with it, or we lose our licences. Of course the rules do get bent. That business with Rumplestiltskin was never satisfactorily explained. (*She cackles*)

1
2 } (*together*) Oh that was you, was it? Goodness.

Maultash We're going to do some rule-bending now. My rose forest needs someone horrid to help keep that awful prince out and you have just offered to do it for me.

$\left.\begin{array}{c} \mathbf{1} \\ \mathbf{2} \end{array}\right\}$ (*together*) Ah, well, we're helpful, rather than horrid and—aaaaaaaah!

They are twisted from afar by Moultash pointing her finger

Maultash You do offer, don't you?

$\left.\begin{array}{c} \mathbf{1} \\ \mathbf{2} \end{array}\right\}$ (*together*) Yes. Yes, please!

Maultash Good. And if you fail—

$\left.\begin{array}{c} \mathbf{1} \\ \mathbf{2} \end{array}\right\}$ (*together*) We won't!

Maultash I will make you play the Final Trick With Time. Hahaha!

$\left.\begin{array}{c} \mathbf{1} \\ \mathbf{2} \end{array}\right\}$ (*together*) What is it?

Maultash I hope you don't find out. Now you will turn into a hideous and vile pair of trees. (*She gestures at 1 and 2*)

1 and 2 totter off

Thunder or music are heard and screams, off

$\left.\begin{array}{c} \mathbf{1} \\ \mathbf{2} \end{array}\right\}$(*together off*) My head is going solid. My arms—they're wooden and stiff. Is that an owl in your upper branches? Aaaah! I'm covered in ivy! Help!

1 and 2 totter back on inside two trees

Maultash Are you truly hideous and vile, or merely shady?

$\left.\begin{array}{c} \mathbf{1} \\ \mathbf{2} \end{array}\right\}$ (*together*) Hideous and vile, hideous and vile.

Maultash More.

1 and 2 stamp about

More.

They stamp about and laugh hollowly

More.

They do more stamping and laughing

All right. Off with you to the forest to work my horrors and make a filthy mess of those dreary Godmothers. Yuk. The very thought of them makes me want to gob. All good people make me want to gob.

1 and 2 exit

Song 17: Maultash's Revenge

(*Singing*) I want revenge on the good!
They've got to be punished for ever and ever.
I'm heartily sick that they should
Be
Terribly pretty and happy and clever.
So
Let me be rid of them now.

Prissy and prim as they seem
I want to destroy them and this is my vow
I'll tickle them all till they scream, ah, ha!
I'll tickle them all till they scream.

(*Speaking; to the Audience*) And you little goody-goodies, sitting out there in your neat rows!

They need a good smack on their bums
And pinching and tweaking with pliers and pinchers
I'd quite like to flatten your thumbs
And shred you to pieces in one of my mincers
I'll relish your grizzles and cries
As I strap everyone to a chair
And dollop hot bacon fat into their eyes
And syrup all over their hair, ah, ha!
And syrup all over their hair

Thunder is heard as Multash and her cloud are wheeled off

SCENE 4

The Magic Rose Forest

Forest music. The lights go up slowly on the Rose Forest. This is unusually thick. It appears to have no roses in it at all, but closer inspection reveals a number of buds—really as many as possible, that are at the moment closed. The lighting is shafty and dank to begin with. There is a terrible silence, marked with just one cicada like sound

Blanche (*off*) This way.
Prince (*off*) It's so tall.

Blanche and the Prince enter. Blanche has a sword

Blanche There we are. The castle's in there somewhere.
Prince What an awful place.
Blanche Yes. Well, here's your sword—Claude.
Prince Thank you.
Blanche Feeling downhearted?
Prince No, no.
Blanche Look, we have met before, haven't we.
Prince No.
Blanche Are you absolutely sure? You can tell me.
Prince We've never met before. Where are the rose flowers?
Blanche You've heard of thornless roses? Well Maultash planted flowerless ones. Typical. However, it seemed to us to be against the rules for spells, so we added some buds which I think you'll find may be helpful later on. Good luck—er—Claude. And Glynis said she did hope you'd overlook her hysterics.

Prince Yes, of course.
Blanche She is over seven thousand now, you know, is Glynis. It's a good
   age, poor dear. Right. Goodbye.

Blanche exits

*A kind of slithering, whispering sound starts, and a voice calls out, low and
seductive, and echoey*

Maultash (*off*) Claude. Claude. Go home Claude, to a nice quiet life.
Prince Is that my dream calling me?

Terrible giggles echo out

Maultash (*off*) No. Go home.
Prince Who is it, then?
Maultash ⎫
1   ⎬ (*together; off*)   (*with mocking repetition*) Who is it, then?
2   ⎭   (*Their giggles turn to laughter*)
Prince Come on, own up. There's someone else in there.
Maultash (*with mocking repetition; off*) There's someone else in there.
Prince Right. Here we go.
Maultash (*with mocking repetition; off*) Here we go.

The Prince wields his sword

   1 and 2, as trees still, dash in and interpose themselves

The Prince's sword breaks and Maultash's laughter rings out

Prince Now what shall I do?
1 Go home.
Prince Never—
2 Home.
Prince I'll force the stems apart with my bare hands.

*The Prince parts the roses and gets a little way in. 1 and 2 begin to operate
"the horrors". For example, a branch or vine suddenly grabs at him and
drags him further, gripping him so he can't escape—1 and 2 operating it like
a rope*

   Stop it. Let me go. Help. I'm stuck.
Maultash (*off*) Yes! (*She laughs*)

*1 and 2, as people in the scenery, pull his hair, they tweak his nose. They
pull his other arm, or leg and pull him in a different direction*

Prince Let go. Let go of me.

*Another branch has a huge dagger-like thorn attached to it. 1 and 2 make it
flail, getting nearer to the Prince all the time. At a crucial moment the Prince
grabs it and wrests it free*

   Oh no, you don't.

The sounds turn to hissing

The Prince extracts himself a little and the vines sway round him. He lashes out with the dagger thorn, and they dodge, or 1 and 2 dodge. There are sounds of distress and anger from the vines and 1 and 2

There! I'll get through.

One of the vines withers under the Prince's attack

2 You won't.
Maultash (*off*) Go back. Go home!
2 We did warn you to keep out, didn't we.

The Prince lashes out towards 1 and 2.

Maultash (*off*) Aaah! Go on. Go. Go.
2 Go on. Go.
Prince (*flailing at 1 and 2*) You aren't going to defeat me, any of you.
Blanche's Voice (*off*) No, they won't defeat you.

Music. Slowly, the flowers lift their buds, the buds open, and reveal the pure white petals of the flowers and the pretty faces of the ladies inside them

Maultash (*off*) Flowers? That's cheating!
A Rose Flower If you have rose bushes, you do have to have roses.
Maultash (*off*) Flowers are yuk.

Song 18: Prince of the Dream

Roses (*singing*)   Prince of the dream,
                               Who has come to his love,
                               Bright are the petals
                               We rain from above.

                               We'll drop our leaves
                               That will show you the way,
                               Prince of the dream
                               Who will bring in the day.

These two verses are repeated in a second great chorus as the petals begin to fall in a great shower

1 Maultash, they're blinding us.
2 We can't see to stop him.
Maultash (*off*) You utterly feeble weeds.
1 They're showing him the way, Maultash.
2 He's finding his way through.
1 And the petals are blinding us.
Maultash (*off*) You slops, you dregs, you shifty swats.

1 and 2 totter off

As the petals fall in a brilliant and continuous stream, backwards and forwards to mark a path, the stems and vines hiss and part to reveal a space lit coolly and clearly. The roses, arranged somehow like a frame, begin to speak

1st Rose There, Prince, can you see the castle now?
Prince Yes, it's exactly how I dreamed it.
2nd Rose Oh, isn't he lovely?
3rd Rose Every inch a prince.
1st Rose Just how I've imagined him, summer after summer.
2nd Rose Where are you prince of, Prince?
Prince Does it matter?
3rd Rose Not to us love, but it might do in there.
Prince I doubt it. Once I get there, it'll be perfect.

Song 18 (reprise)

Roses

Prince of the dream
Who has come from afar
Still you will need
To explain who you are.

Prince

I am the prince
Who has known all his life
That Rose of the forest castle
Will be his wife.

At the end of the song the Prince exits

SCENE 5

The Final Trick With Time

Maultash enters with 1 and 2. She is berating 1 and 2 who are still in their tree outfits

Maultash You utter maunge-pots, you haddocks, you sausage meat.
1
2 } *(together)* We're terribly sorry, Maultash.
1 We tried to be frightful and macho.
2 We tried to be horrid he-men.
Maultash *(calling upwards)* Clock! Clock of Clocks! I want the Clock of Clocks for the final trick with time!
1 Oh, look, Maultash, the Clock of Clocks.

A vast clock, or part of it, comes down. The great hands are moving towards 100

2 The Clock of Clocks for the final trick with time.
Maultash *(to the Audience)* Don't think the Prince is going to reach the palace, because he isn't. *(To 1 and 2)* Clear off. I don't want you spoiling things again.
1
2 } *(together)* We'll go over there and watch what you do.
Yes, we'll go over there while you do the final trick.

Maultash I'll make time go backwards so the Prince will never reach the castle.

The Prince enters

Prince I shall just be in nice time. The hundred years is up in five minutes. There! You can see it on the clock.

Maultash Now!

There is a flash in the clock. The hand stops and then begins to go the other way

Prince !Clock that on it see can you. There! Minutes five in up is years hundred the. Time nice in be just shall I.

He walks backwards off the stage

1 and 2 walk back on in their tree outfits

2 Trick final the do you while, there over go we'll, yes.

Glynis enters

Glynis Stop! Stop time!

The clock stops. 1 and 2 are frozen to the spot

That's cheating.

Maultash No it isn't. The spell said "when a hundred years is up". It said nothing about the hundred years *never* being up. Oh, you need the mind of a lawyer for this business.

Glynis Foul, foul you, Maultash.

Maultash Yes. And I'm going to put the clock back to when there was no Princess at all. (*She laughs, burps and belches*) Oh yes, I will.

Audience Oh no, you won't.

Continue Audience participation

Glynis (*to the Audience*) Look, this is really serious. Help us, please, to get the Prince into the palace. Don't you know a song to make time pass somehow? To make time go the right way? (*She asks for the songsheet*)

Song 9: Tick tock (reprise)

Tick tock tick tock
Time is passing round the clock
Days and nights and weeks and years
Time is never still.

Glynis leads the Audience in the round

1 and 2 go back, waver and then go to the point at which they hide

Maultash (*at intervals as the round goes on*) Stop it. Don't make that noise. I'll turn you into toads.

Glynis No, you won't.
Maultash Yes I will. etc.
Glynis There you are, very well done. I'd like to congratulate you.

Then the clock starts going backwards again. 1 and 2 start moving backwards

Oh, help.

Great efforts are needed to stop 1 and 2 and get them back. The round is stopped. Once again 1 and 2 go back. Once again the round is started. This can go on for as long as is wanted, finishing with 1 and 2 leaving the stage.

Finally the singers get the Prince across the stage and the clock strikes one vast bell-like tone as it reaches 100

That's it! We've done it! The hundred years is over, Maultash.
Maultash Oh, nettles! Dandelions and old handkerchiefs. (*She snaps her broomstick*) Oh, I don't think I should've done that.

1 and 2 enter, free of their tree outfits

1 No, you shouldn't have. We're free now.
2 And full of nonsense.

1 and 2 skip away like wild things

Maultash Drat and bloomers! I haven't finished yet!

Maultash exits

Glynis But she's no use without her broomstick, none at all. Thank you ever so much for helping. I'm not a fool you see, Blanche. I'm not a fool.

Black-out

SCENE 6

The Final Moments in the Royal Palace

The courtyard. Everyone is asleep and snoring. Dust and cobwebs are every-where. Prince Claude is gazing at them

Prince Here they are, still asleep even though the hundred years is up.

Song 19: Will It Come True?

(*Singing*) Will it come true,
Now that it's over
Will she be mine
Just how she seemed
All that I've wanted to hold
And all that I've dreamed

> And will there be love
> Now and forever
> Fresh as the spring
> Warming as May
> Bright as the light in her eyes
> Never fading away
> Will a kiss wake the day.
>
> She—calling me onwards
> Me—here for her sake
> Both of us loving and living awake.

He moves on to the Princess

Rose. The Princess Rose. As beautiful as she was when I first saw her in my dreams.

He kneels and kisses her. Bells, "Prince of the Dream" music. A general stirring but it is Rose who wakes up first, yawns and gazes on the Prince

Rose   Oh, Crispin! (*She hugs him*) How lovely to see you. I've been asleep.
Prince   Yes, I'm Claude, actually.
Rose   What?
Prince   Claude.
Rose (*laughing*)   No, you're not. You're Crispin. did you get the daisies?
Claude   What daisies?
King (*waking*)   Where are those point inspectors?
Rose   Father.
King   Rose?
Rose   We're saved. It's over.
Archbishop   They must've put something in the porridge.
Nurse   Oh woe, woe and misery! It's all my fault, I shouldn't have let her go out of my sight.
Queen   Hallowpenny, I have the impression you have said that before.
Nurse   Cynthia?
Queen   I *beg* your pardon?
Nurse   I'm so sorry, Your Majesty. I don't know what came over me.
Rose   Mother, Father, Hallowpenny, everyone! Everything's all right. The hundred years must be over and Crispin has come and made it all completely better, haven't you. In your funny clothes.
Nurse   I knew it. Oh, Crispin. (*She smothers him in a kiss*) You treasure of a lambkin boy!
Prince (*crossly*)   My name is Claude. Really, it's Claude.
King   Oh, Crispin, you splendid fellow, despite your comic get-up. Well done, well done, well done.
Queen   Very good, Crispin.
Nurse   Oh, I knew we could depend on Crispin from the moment I first saw him. Mind you, it was the way he was brought up that made the difference.
Queen   If you're not gloomy, you're cocky, aren't you.

Nurse Did you bring the Prince with you, love, show him the way, did you?

Rose Oh never mind the Prince, I expect he's awfully stuck up.

Claude No he isn't. He's me.

Nurse Who's you?

Rose He must've given me a kiss of course. It might be nice to meet him.

Prince I gave you the kiss.

Rose (*laughing*) Oh, don't be silly.

Queen You're only a stable boy.

Nurse What's wrong with stable boys?

Prince I'm a Prince, my name is Claude, and I fought my way through a forest of roses.

King What forest of roses?

Prince Well, it's disappeared now, but—

King Are you telling lies, Crispin?

Nurse No, he is not! Crispin never tells lies!

Rose No, he doesn't. He's my best friend.

1 and 2 enter

1 Your Majesty.

2 Your delightful Majesty.

1 If we could just most helpfully explain ...

King Are you the point inspectors?

1
2 } (*together*) Yes, your Majesty.

King You're fired.

1
2 } (*together*) But, Your Majesty ...

The Godmothers enter

Blanche Oh, for goodness sake, you mortals are absolute fools. Now will you please understand. This is a prince.

Rose Crispin?

All express amazement or disbelief

Blanche Tell them, Roxy.

Roxy Well he is a prince. And the reason why he looks like Crispin is because ...

Maultash enters

Maultash Turn into toads, all of you!

King I beg your pardon?

Maultash attempts a spell. Nothing happens

Maultash Oh knickers.

Maultash exits

Glynis (*calling*) No good without your broomstick.

Blanche And you've lost your licence.

King She reminded me of someone we know.

Queen I think she's got one of those unpleasant diseases other people catch. (*Calling off*) Give her some money, will you?

1 It was Maultash, your Majesty.

2 It was the awful lady herself.

King You're fired.

Rose To me your're still Crispin, Crispin.

Queen (*to Rose*) Come away from Crispin, there's a dear.

Prince I've come from far over the sea, I've fought all sorts of things and forests and—

Queen What was nice for children is quite different for grown ups.

Nurse (*to the Queen*) Now listen here . . .

Rose He is my friend, Mother. Just remember that, please.

Queen Where's the prince who kissed you?

Glynis He's the prince who kissed her.

Blanche He really is.

Roxy And the reason he looks . . .

All What?

King Why didn't someone say?

1 We knew he was a prince, Your Majesty, and we we're trying to—

King You're fired.

Crispin Thank you for explaining, ladies. Now if you'll all just go . . .

Rose Wait a minute. Go on Roxy. I want to get this straight. Roxy, tell us more.

Roxy Well, there's quite a lot to explain. When Maultash's silly forest grew, Crispin stayed outside and—

Maultash enters with a football rattle

Maultash A pack of lies. Don't believe a word. That man is really a sea serpent.

King Archbishop, exorcise this thing, will you? I do believe it's all that's left of Maultash.

Archbishop Certainly, Your Majesty. What fun. (*He puts some spells on Maultash*)

Maultash Oh, go jump on your crozier.

Maultash exits

Archbishop I do hate people who won't play.

Rose Now, go on.

Nurse Yes, please go on, er . . . er . . .

Roxy Roxy.

Nurse Roxy.

Roxy Well, one day when Crispin had wandered far and wide, he saved a princess in distress and . . .

Maultash enters beating a gong

Maultash All fairy stories. Don't listen.

All Oh go away. Do shut up.
Glynis You're a has-been.
Maultash *I'm* a has-been!
Queen I've given you money. What else do you want?
Maultash Revenge. (*She beats the gong louder*)

Everyone covers their ears

Blanche I've been wanting to do this for years.

Blanche points her wand at Maultash. Maultash jumps and screams and the gong explodes

Maultash Blanche, you're a spoilsport.
Blanche Maultash, you're a threat to the environment.
Nurse Now sit down and be quiet.
Maultash (*imitating Nurse*) Now sit down and be quiet.
Blanche Go on, Roxy.
Rose Yes. (*To the Prince*) I warn you—whoever you are. I'm not marrying you just because you woke me up.
Roxy Anyway, Crispin married this princess and so he became a prince and his son became a prince and his grandson, turned out to be—
Maultash Boring, boring, boring, boring, boring.
Nurse You'll have a dose of syrup of figs if you're not quiet this minute.
Roxy His grandson turned out to be Claude. This person. There!
All He's Crispin's grandson?
Roxy Yes. And that's really, really nice.
Rose Well, I do see it's sort of interesting.
Queen And pretty amazing.
Maultash Yuk!
Roxy And actually Crispin's father was a prince, too.
Glynis How d'you know?
Roxy I just do.
Nurse I always knew Crispin wouldn't give in, young man, and I'm sure you won't give in either. I'm more or less your great grandmother as a matter of fact.

Roxy smirks to herself

Queen At least it means they can go on being friends.
Rose Yes, it does mean that.
Nurse Oh yes, don't they look lovely?
Prince Yes, we do. And actually, it wouldn't matter if I wasn't a prince because ...
Rose We'll stay friends forever. Just like Crispin and I were.

The Prince kisses Rose properly

All Oh!
Nurse Oh!
Rose (*coming out of the kiss*) Oh!

Archbishop Your Majesty! There's a stable boy been kissing your daughter!

King He's a prince, Archbishop. Haven't you been listening?

Archbishop Oh, then it's all right.

Nurse And that kiss was a happy-ever-after kiss if ever I saw one.

King Was it.

Rose Yes, it was.

Nurse (*to the King*) Did you ever say call me Bobby?

Queen No, he didn't.

Rose Oh, Claude! We must be in love after all! How extraordinary!

Prince At last!

Rose At last.

The Prince and Rose hug each other

Nurse Aren't they just lovely? Any sign of my own true love, by the by?

Godmothers Sorry, sorry.

Glynis I've tried very hard to find one for you, because I do understand the plight of the single woman.

Blanche Oh, Glynis, really.

Nurse Well in that case, I'm going to settle down with the Archbishop and look after his mitre.

Roxy Oh, lovely!

Archbishop Elizabeth.

Nurse Tarquin.

Blanche As for you, Maultash ...

Maultash As for me, I'm going to go on making life interesting for people like I always did.

Nurse Oh dear.

King And if I'm not mistaken, that seems to be that. (*To 1 and 2*) You two are fired, of course—

All Oh, no. No. No. They're all right.

King Well, they did let the spinning wheel—

Nurse Oh don't fuss, your Majesty. Issue a proclamation that we're all going to live happily ever after.

1 ⎫ (*together*) A proclamation! Everyone, a proclamation! (*They pull out*
2 ⎭   *trumpets and blow a very fancy piece*)

The King takes out a proclamation and this leads into the final chorus

Song 20: Just Good Friends

King (*singing*)   The time has come to make this proclamation
                         To the anxious and long suffering nation.
                         The Princess Rose and Claude have now decided

Rose   (*Chorus*) That they will never be divided.
                         We're just good friends,
                         Starting out together,
                         You can bet you're never on your own.

With Good Good Friends,
Weathering the weather's
Better when together than alone.

When your luck is running out,
Take a great big breath and shout,
For Good Good Friends. 'Cos
That's what love is about.

Prince

Just Good Friends.
It's not imagination
That's making all my dreams come true,
Just Good Friends,
That's the situation,
And all you ever have to be is you.

Prince
Rose } (*together*)

And for everybody here
We'd just like to make it clear,
That at the end we're
Just Good Friends.

All

When you're really blue
Nothing you can do
To brighten up your day.
Friends come around
Pick you off the ground
'N' chase those clouds away.
And if you really want the key
To a great eternity,
It's Good Good Friends,
'Cos that's what love should be.

Nurse

Just Good Friends,
Now I've found my true love—
I'll be true to you until the end.

Archbishop

Just Good Friends,
Think what we can do, love,
In the happy hours we shall spend.

Nurse
Archbishop
Nurse } (*together*)
Archbishop
Blanche

I'll be weaving at my loom.
By your window I shall croon.
The perfect blend as
Just Good Friends.
When you're really low
And you're feeling so
Sorry for yourself,
Make a wish and

	We're in a position
	To bring you back to health.
Godmothers	With a twinkle and a sigh,
	We'll be there to dry your eye
	On us depend,
	We're just Good Friends.

King
Queen *(together)*

All Good Friends
Have a little hiccough
But they always pick up in the end.

1 and 2

Some Good Friends
Tend to get our wick up,
The ones that drive us screaming round the bend.

K and Q
1 and 2 *(together)*

We give no names at all,
But watch where our eyes fall.
Still at the end
We're all Good Friends.

Maultash

Just you wait
I'll make you squirm.
You'll be bait
For my pet worm.
Or I'll turn you into snails,
And make you eat rat's tails.
But let's pretend
We're all Good Friends.

Dance routine

All

Just Good Friends
Starting out together
You can bet you're never on your own
With Good Good Friends
Weathering the weather's
Better altogether than alone
And we'd like to say once more
In a long and loud encore
That at the end, we're
Just Good Friends.

CURTAIN

FURNITURE AND PROPERTY LIST

Only essential properties etc are listed here. Further dressing may be added at the producer's discretion

PROLOGUE

Frontcloth

ACT 1

SCENE 1

On stage: Standing set of castle
Dressing as desired
Large Royal pram or cot

Personal: **Godmothers:** wands (used throughout play)

SCENE 2

On stage: As Scene 1 with addition of two thrones

Off stage: Suitcases (**Nurse**)
Baby (**1 and 2**)
Folding table (**1 and 2**)
Clean nappy, cotton wool, bottle of milk etc (**1 and 2**)

Personal: **King:** scroll

SCENE 3

On stage: Christening robe
Off stage: Marvellous perambulator (can be same as for Scene 1)
Cardboard box. *In it:* baby (**Roxy**)

SCENE 4

Off stage: Sharpness disposal unit
Items for disposal (as indicated in text)

Personal: **Glynis:** fairy dust
Roxy: piece of paper
Blanche: fairy dust
Maultash: broomstick (used throughout play)

SCENE 5

Frontcloth. Clock and song sheet (**Stage Management**)

SCENE 6

On stage: Garden plants, shrubs etc including rose bush
Off stage: Thistle exterminator (**1 and 2**)
Prickle container (**1 and 2**)

Scene 7

No properties required

Scene 8

On stage:	Flags, bunting, banners Tower (on truck if possible). *In it:* spinning wheel Table or box with Rose's handkerchief in it
Off stage:	Bunch of daisies (**Crispin**)
Personal:	Trumpets

ENTR'ACTE

No properties required

ACT II

Scene 1

On stage:	As Act 1, Scene 8

No properties required

Scene 2

No properties required

Scene 3

Off stage:	Two tree outfits (**1 and 2**)

Scene 4

On stage:	Rose forest. Tightly budded roses which open in the scene to reveal white petals and ladies' faces in the centres
Personal:	**Blanche:** sword

Scene 5

Off stage:	Clock (**Stage Management**) Songsheet (**Stage Management**)

Scene 6

Personal:	**Maultash:** football rattle, gong **1 and 2:** trumpets **King:** proclamation

LIGHTING PLOT

PROLOGUE

To open: House Lights on

Cue 1 As 1 and 2 go to the stage (Page 1)
Begin to dim House Lights

Cue 2 **1:** "Can we lower the lights, please?" (Page 1)
Take out House Lights completely

ACT I, SCENE 1

To open: Night lighting

Cue 3 **Courtier:** "... best of family life?" (Page 6)
Fade to Black-out

ACT I, SCENE 2

To open: Dawn lighting. Shaft of light for Godmother's entrance

Cue 4 Archbishop enters (Page 9)
Light increases to morning

Cue 5 **King and Queen:** "Yuk, yuk, yuk, yuk, yuk." (Page 13)
Black-out

ACT I, SCENE 3 and SCENE 4

To open: General interior light

Cue 6 As Scene 4 opens (Page 16)
"Magical" lighting

Cue 7 As Maultash enters (Page 17)
Green spot on Maultash

Cue 8 **Maultash:** "... some very nasty deeds." (Page 18)
Flash of lightning

Cue 9 Nurse ceases being paralysed (Page 18)
Flash of lightning

Cue 10 **Maultash:** "... christenings, I really do!" (Page 19)
Flash of lightning

Cue 11 **Courtier:** "... absolutely miserable." (Page 22)
Black-out

ACT I, SCENE 5

To open: Front cloth lit

Cue 12 **Glynis:** "Well done!" (Page 22)
Black-out

ACT I, SCENE 6

To open:	Exterior lighting	
Cue 13	**Crispin:** "... really feel about it?" *Black-out*	(Page 26)

ACT I, SCENE 7

To open:	Spot on Rose	
Cue 14	At end of song *Black-out*	(Page 27)

ACT I, SCENE 8

To open:	Exterior lighting	
Cue 15	As tower moves forward *Light inside of tower*	(Page 30)
Cue 16	**Maultash:** "Your daughter's dying." *Take out tower lights*	(Page 30)
Cue 17	**Roxy:** "... tell you what's happened." *Fade to night level*	(Page 30)

ENTR'ACTE

Cue 18	1;"House lights out. Follow spot." *Take out house lights. Follow spot on Prince and 1 and 2*	(Page 33)

ACT II, SCENE 1

To open:	"Mysterious" lighting	
Cue 19	As everyone goes into their bodies *Fade "mysterious" lighting*	(Page 42)

ACT II, SCENE 2

To open:	Frontcloth lit
No cues	

ACT II, SCENE 3

To open:	Cloudy, thundery lighting
No cues	

ACT II, SCENE 4

To open:	Shafts of dank lighting
No cues	

Act II, Scene 5

To open:	General lighting	
Cue 20	**Maultash:** "Now!"	(Page 50)
	Flash in clock	
Cue 21	**Glynis:** "I'm not a fool"	(Page 51)
	Black-out	

Act II, Scene 6

To open:	General exterior lighting
No cues	

EFFECTS PLOT

PROLOGUE

Cue 1	**1:** "... into the world for His Majesty." *Infant cries*	(Page 2)
Cue 2	**2:** "Rejoice!" *Bells, guns, crashes*	(Page 2)
Cue 3	**1 and 2:** "A princess! Delicious!" *Bells, guns etc*	(Page 3)

ACT I

Cue 4	As Scene 1 opens *Continue bangs and bells and increase infant crying*	(Page 4)
Cue 5	1 and 2 get Audience to participate *Crying increases*	(Page 5)
Cue 6	**Courtier:** "A nanny." *Cries stop*	(Page 5)
Cue 7	As Princess is put into her cot *Screams*	(Page 6)
Cue 8	As 1 and 2 bring baby on *Crying, gurgling as per script*	(Page 10)
Cue 9	**Nurse:** "Windies for nanny panny." *Burp, followed by gurgles*	(Page 10)
Cue 10	Nurse hugs baby *Gurgles*	(Page 13)
Cue 11	**Roxy:** "... ever so lovely." *Coos, gurgles*	(Page 14)
Cue 12	**Godmothers** (*singing*); "Here is Roxy ..." *Jet aeroplane roar. Crash.*	(Page 17)
Cue 13	**Maultash:** "... some very nasty deeds." *Explosion*	(Page 18)
Cue 14	Nurse ceases being paralysed *Thunder*	(Page 18)
Cue 15	**Maultash:** "... christenings, I really do!" *Explosion, roar of aeroplane*	(Page 19)
Cue 16	1 topples King's crown in SDU *Grinding noise*	(Page 21)
Cue 17	As each item is put into SDU *Repeat grinding noise*	(Page 21)
Cue 18	As clock reaches 16 *Alarm sounds*	(Page 22)
Cue 19	**Maultash:** "Just you wait." *Roar of broomstick*	(Page 31)

| *Cue* 20 | As lights fade to night
Owl hoots | (Page 32) |

ACT II

Cue 21	After song 15 *Wind and thunder, continue through Scene 3*	(Page 43)
Cue 22	1 and 2 totter off *Thunder (or music)*	(Page 45)
Cue 23	At end of Song 17 *Thunder*	(Page 46)
Cue 24	As Scene 4 opens *Cicada sound*	(Page 46)
Cue 25	Blanche exits *Slithering, whispering sounds*	(Page 47)
Cue 26	**Prince:**"Oh no, you don't." *Hissing noise*	(Page 47)
Cue 27	As Prince gets across stage *Clock tolls as it reaches 100*	(Page 51)
Cue 28	As Prince kisses Rose *Bells*	(Page 52)
Cue 29	**Maultash** jumps and screams *Gong explodes*	(page 55)